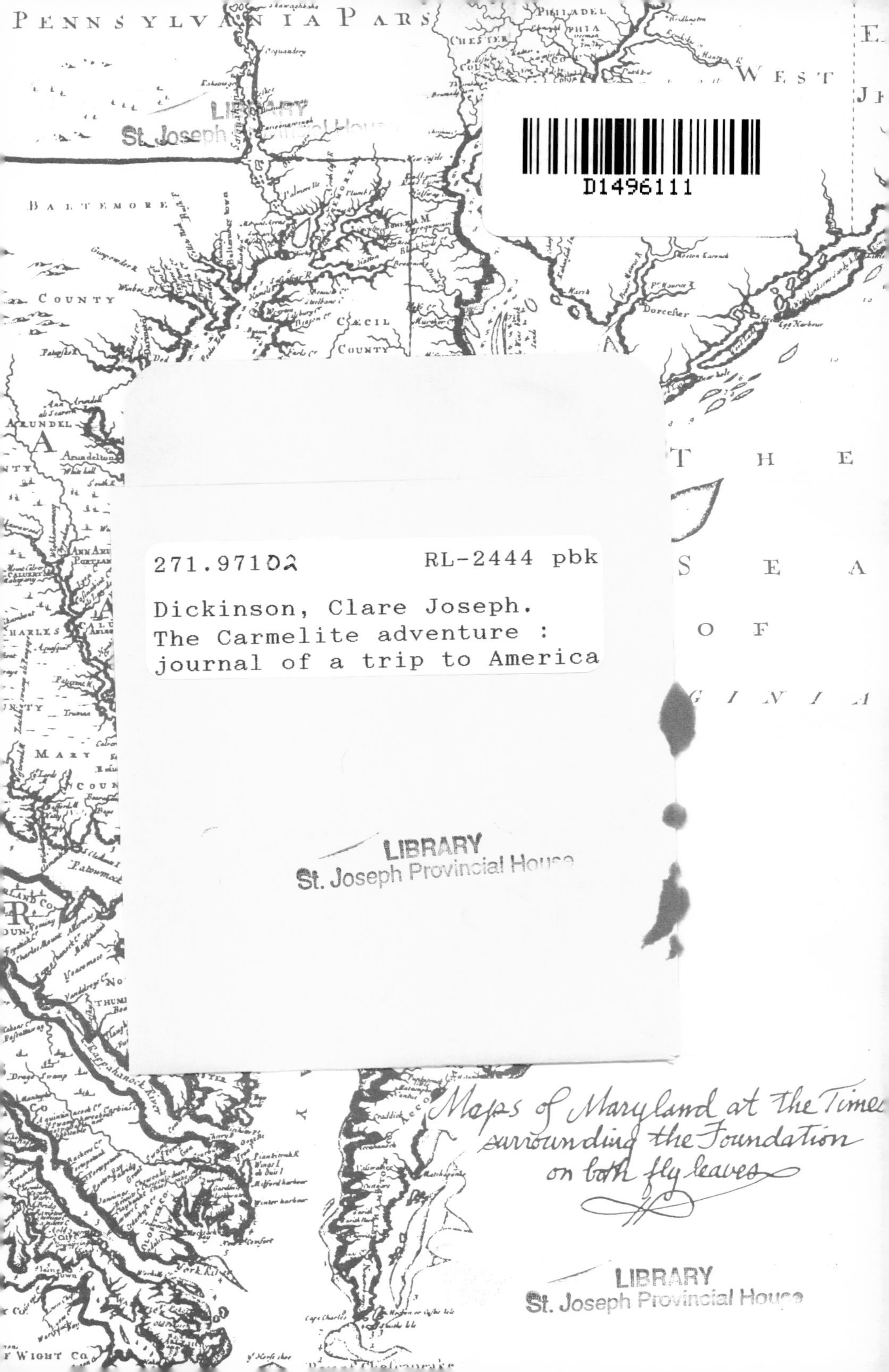
PENNSYLVANIA PARS
BALTEMORE
COUNTY
CECIL
COUNTY
CHESTER
WEST
Dorcester
THE
SEA
OF
Patowmack
Rappahanock River
York R.
Maps of Maryland at the Times surrounding the Foundation on both fly leaves

CARMELITE SOURCES

VOLUME II

THE CARMELITE ADVENTURE

Clare Joseph Dickinson's

Journal of A Trip To America and Other Documents

Edited by Constance FitzGerald, O.C.D.

Illustrated and Designed by Marie-Celeste Fadden, O.C.D.

Printed by Reno Carmel

Published by Carmelite Sisters
Baltimore, MD

Gratitude to Dolores Liptak, R.S.M., Joseph P. Chinnici, O.F.M., Robert Emmett Curran, S.J., Thomas W. Spalding, C.F.X., Patricia Scanlan, O.C.D., and the Carmelites of Baltimore and Reno.

Partially funded by a grant from the Maryland Humanities Council

THE CARMELITE ADVENTURE

Co-Publisher Carmelite Communities Associated

LIBRARY OF CONGRESS CATALOG CARD NUMBER: 90-80681

ISBN 0-9624104-1-1

To

Thomas M. Kilduff, O.C.D.

our brother and friend

who travelled many miles with us

on the

American Carmelite journey.

CONTENTS

INTRODUCTION

On April 19, 1790, four Carmelite nuns and one Jesuit-trained priest[1] set out on a journey from Hoogstraet in Belgium to Charles County, Maryland in North America. The nuns were members of English-speaking communities in Hoogstraet and Antwerp, important centers for the English recusant community of the Lowlands in the seventeenth and eighteenth centuries. All but one of the nuns were natives of Maryland descended from the Catholic gentry reaching back to the beginning of Lord Baltimore's colony. Accompanied by their Maryland-born chaplain, the nuns were going to establish the first community of religious women in the thirteen original states. The journal of their voyage, written in the hand of Clare Joseph Dickinson, provides us with a woman's view of eighteenth century ocean travel.

HISTORICAL ROOTS

The Carmelite Order they were establishing in the new world had weathered nearly six centuries of existence since its eremitical beginnings on Mount Carmel in Palestine at the dawn of the thirteenth century.[2] Carmelite friars had migrated to Europe and joined the great mendicant surge; they had moved into the city and the university, striking an uneasy balance between contemplation and apostolic ministry, between desert and city.[3] The long affiliation of women with the Order had been formally recognized in 1452 when the beguines of "Ten Elsen" in Guelders were received into the Order by John Soreth, the General.[4] The Counter Reformation had seen the reform of both the nuns and the friars initiated in Spain in 1562 by Teresa of Avila. During her life time, seventeen convents of Carmelite nuns of the Reform had been founded throughout Spain setting the stage for the separation of the Carmelites into two distinct Orders by 1593.[5] When Teresa died in 1582, she left not only a way of contemplative life in the post-Tridentine Church but also a deep conviction about the place of contemplative prayer in the transformation of the world. Together with John of the Cross, who had worked with her in the reform of the friars, she bequeathed to the Carmelite Order and to Christianity a legacy of mystical texts that bear extraordinary witness to the experience of God in human life.

It was the disciples and successors of St. Teresa of Avila, Anne of Jesus (Lobera) and Anne of St. Bartholomew (Garcia), who carried the Teresian tradition to the Low Countries and the Continent. Only twenty-two years after the great reformer's death, they accepted the invitation of Cardinal de Berulle and crossed the Pyrenees to found monasteries in Paris (1604), Pontoise (1605), Dijon (1605) and Tours (1608). By 1607, Anne of Jesus had moved into the Spanish Netherlands to found "the Royal Convent" in Brussels. In quick succession "the Spanish Mothers" made foundations in Louvain (1607), Mons (1608), Antwerp (1612) and Mechlin (1616). From these houses in the Low Countries Anne of Jesus chose five Carmelites for the task of founding an English-speaking Carmel. Led by Anne of the Ascension (Worsley, 1588-1644), they established in 1619 a Carmel in Antwerp, on the rue Houblonniere in Hopland.[6] To this monastery, which had the character of a motherhouse, and to its two English-speaking daughter houses of Lierre (1648) and Hoogstraet (1678), came women from recusant families in England and the Lowlands.[7]

Many of these familes had forfeited property and wealth to practice their religion freely in the Low Countries. Others, to remain Catholics, had risked imprisonment and even death in their native England. The English-speaking Carmelites by inheritance, therefore, prized liberty of conscience and freedom of religion.

It was not until 1742 that British colonials from Maryland began crossing the ocean to become Carmelites.[8] In that year Anna Maria Parnham (1716-1784) entered the monastery in Lierre. She was followed by Eleanor Wharton (1723-1793) and Jane Brooke (-1771) in 1749, Mary Boone (1718-1758) in 1750 and Anne Boone (1733-1811) in 1760.[9] Mary Brent (1731-1784) and her cousin Margaret Pye (1724-1777) joined the Antwerp community in 1751; three years later Anne Matthews (1732-1800) and Ann Hill (1734-1813) entered the community in Hoogstraet.[10]

By the last quarter of the eighteenth century, therefore, the seed for Carmel in America had taken root and produced strong American leadership for the English Teresians in Hoogstraet, Antwerp and Lierre. This leadership proved to be a strong base from which to plan for the founding of a new monastery in Maryland.

FOUNDERS:

MARY MARGARET BRENT

To understand the foundation of the first community of women religious in the thirteen original states, one must look, first of all, at the founder who did not return to her homeland: Mother Mary Margaret Brent who died in 1784 at age fifty-three just after completing six years as prioress of the Antwerp community. With Mother Bernardina Matthews, a neighbor from Charles County who was prioress at Hoogstraet Carmel from 1771 to 1790, Mary Margaret Brent had planned the first Carmelite foundation in their native Maryland.

Mary Brent was born into the Maryland Catholic elite on September 1, 1731 at "Brentfield" in Charles County. She was the first of eight children, only four of whom lived beyond infancy. Her mother, Mary Wharton (-1773/4), was the daughter of Henry Wharton and Jane Doyne whose brother, Jesse Doyne, also married a Brent.[11] When Mary's father, Robert Brent, married Mary Wharton on May 6, 1729 at Durham Church, Trinity parish, in Charles County, he moved from Virginia to "Brentfield." It was there sixty-one years later, on July 11, 1790, that the sloop carrying the first four Carmelites up the Chesapeake and Potomac rivers would dock at Brent's Landing near the home of Mary Brent's brother, Bobby Brent. Like his sister, he was not to participate in the foundation itself. He had died on January 6, 1790 just six months before the nuns' arrival.

Mary's father, Robert Brent (1704-1750), was born at Woodstock in Stafford County, Virginia. He was the grandson of George Brent who emigrated to the colonies in 1670 and settled at Woodstock near his uncle, Giles Brent, who had moved from Maryland to Virginia after a dispute with Lord Baltimore.[12] Giles, Foulke and their sisters Margaret and Mary, a collateral Brent family, were the first of a long line of Maryland and Virginia Brents to emigrate to America. In 1637 they settled in Maryland and accumulated vast landholdings under the proprietary laws of the colony.

Margaret Brent (1601-1671), called "gentleman" in the records because of her influence as a landowner, administrator and attorney, was one of the largest landowners in Maryland. At Governor Leonard Calvert's death she became not only the executor of his estate but also Lord Baltimore's administrator in the colony. As Cecil Calvert's attorney and in view of her own landholdings, she requested in 1648 a vote in the Maryland Assembly.[13] This strong, fearless woman was Mary Brent's great, great, great aunt.

Heir to this kind of legacy, Mary Brent was ripe for the adventure and challenge of a religious vocation and all it entailed. Although probably unable to pursue an education abroad as the sons of the wealthy Catholic gentry did, she did not hesitate to accept the hazards of an ocean voyage and a lifetime separation from her family in pursuit of her life's goals.[14] Her parents, however, were reluctant to part with their oldest child as an account written at the time of her death poignantly demonstrates:

> Her father...could not find it in his heart to yeald his consent [to her vocation]... till at length, overcome by importunity, he tore from his heart, to offer in sacrifice to God, the dearest object of his Paternal love; the time prefixt for her departure her Father fearing anything should be wanting, on the journey, furnished the ship for her use with every sort of provission: as Gees, Turkeys, Chickins, Hogs, sheep, and corn for their food, chocolete, tea, coffe, suger, dryed fruit, and infine - everything his tenderness for her brought into his mind.[15]

A narrative written by the Hoogstraet Carmelites concerning Mary's entrance at Antwerp suggests that the loss of his daughter hastened Robert Brent's death. He died at forty-six years of age on February 4, 1750 while she was crossing the ocean to Europe.[16] Knowledge of these deep family bonds may shed light on the development of Mary Margaret Brent's spirituality, particularly her experience of God's love, the importance of the Sacred Heart, and her balanced attitudes concerning authority.

Mary Brent was eighteen years old when, accompanied by her cousin, Margaret Pye, she made the voyage to join the English Teresians in Antwerp. A young man on board the ship tried, with some success, to win her heart:

> The enimie envious of her approaching happiness, laid snares in her way to hinder her pious designes, putting into the heart of a young gentleman, who was embarked on the vessell, to try by constancy, and affection, that she at length told him, that in case

> she did not succeed in her holy pretentions, he should have the prefferance in her regards to any other.[17]

The profession records of the Antwerp Community indicate Mary made her vows as Mary Margaret of the Angels on October 10, 1751 after receiving the sacrament of confirmation from the Bishop of Antwerp, Dominic de Ghentis.[18] She was twenty years old. It is further recorded that she was a "native of America in the County of Maryland."

That she was important to the foundation of Carmel in America is evident from the Brent materials the founders brought with them from Antwerp to Southern Maryland. Although Mother Mary Margaret Brent had already been dead six years by the time the project was put into effect, the founders remembered their intention of having her as the first prioress. Still inspired by her memory and her dreams, they brought with them materials she had written or organized. Some recorded the history of the superiors of Antwerp and Hoogstraet Carmels; others the anniversaries of the deaths of the nuns of Antwerp from 1678 to 1784. More importantly, for the sake of posterity, they brought several of her treasured books and some original papers that were indicative of her rich spirituality.

BERNARDINA MATTHEWS

When Mary Margaret Brent died, it fell to her close collaborator, Mother Bernardina Matthews in Hoogstraet, to take on the task of leading the new foundation. Through her the tradition of both colonial Maryland Catholicism and Carmelite life and spirituality would be passed to a new generation. Like Mary Margaret Brent, Bernardina Matthews combined family heritage, experience and natural skills to provide the kind of leadership that would guarantee a future for the American Teresian foundation.

Anne Matthews' family had been in Maryland since

the first years of the Maryland colony. Her great grandfather, Dr. Thomas Matthews (1622-1676), emigrated from England to Maryland between 1636 and 1638.[19] Anne, who was born in Charles County in 1732, was one of three children born to Joseph Matthews and Susanna Craycroft. Anne's father died when she was only two years old leaving a 345 acre farm, a sparsely furnished house and two slaves.[20] The family situation was improved, in both 1734 and 1741, when her mother received legacies from the estate of her father, Ignatius Craycroft. By 1741, Anne's mother had married Edward Clements. Even though Anne became a Carmelite nun, she was not forgotten in Maryland. Seventeen years after she left her home, her somewhat misinformed uncle, Benjamin Craycroft, bequeathed slaves to her with the understanding that they would be sold and the money sent to her "in France at the Nunnery of Poor Clares."[21]

Each of Anne Matthews' brothers had a significant role to play in the foundation of Carmel in America. Her oldest brother, William, was the father of Susanna and Ann Teresa Matthews who in 1786 joined their aunt in the Carmel of Hoogstraet. Although they were professed only two and a half years, Sisters Mary Eleanora and Mary Aloysia Matthews became members of the founding party. They had come to the Lowlands in the hope of bringing Carmel to Maryland and the Hoogstraet community probably understood that their influential family ties augured well for the success of the new foundation. Having seen so many of their daughters depart for convents in Europe, the Maryland Catholic gentry had been waiting a long time for the opportunity to bring religious life for women to the colonies.

It was Anne's second brother, Ignatius, who, sometime after the Revolutionary War, wrote the formal invitation to his sister urging her to return to Maryland: "Now is your time to found in this country for peace is declared and religion is free."[22] Ignatius Matthews (1730-1790) was ordained at the English College in Vallodolid in 1763 before entering the Jesuit novitiate at Watten in the Lowlands. He was back in Maryland by 1766 acting as pastor of the Newtown and Deer Creek congregations. Destined not to share in the foundation he urged upon his sister, he died May 11, 1790 while Mother Bernardina was on the high seas, coming to found Carmel in America.[23]

While undocumented narratives of Hoogstraet Carmel assume Anne's education as a child in Europe, there is no more evidence for this than there was in Mary Margaret Brent's case. Nevertheless, Anne Matthews was certainly literate in both English and French. Accompanied by Ann Hill, she sailed for the Low Countries in 1754, probably for the first time. She was twenty-two years old. In the monastery of Our Lady of Sicham, Hoogstraet, she received the religious habit September 30, 1754 with the name Bernardina Teresa Xavier of St. Joseph. The following year she made her profession.[24] It seems that the community was aware of Bernardina's exceptional gifts from the beginning of her religious life since she was appointed mistress of novices at the completion of her own novitiate. In 1771, when she was thirty-nine years of age, she was elected prioress of the community.

The Hoogstraet tradition makes clear that Mother Bernardina was greatly loved as a prioress and respected as a capable administrator. Graced with unusual contemplative perception, she was revered by her sisters as a wise spiritual guide. Her friend and successor as prioress of Hoogstraet, Ann Hill, wrote to her cousin, Bishop John Carroll:

> The grief as well as the great loss we have sustained in parting with so valuable and much esteemed a superior, is greater than I can express... [I] must own...that myself and community have made the greatest sacrifice

we possibly could in parting with its worthy foundress.[25]

That Bernardina, herself, was rooted in and deeply loved the community she led for nineteen years is evident in some of the papers she brought to Maryland. A list of the names of the Hoogstraet sisters with their various anniversaries and a careful floor plan of the Hoogstraet monastery in her own hand reveal her desire to keep the community she left clearly etched in her memory. Even more telling are the materials which disclose the formative influences that shaped her Carmelite life and spirituality: "The Secrets of A Religious Life Disclos'd To A Novice By Her Spiritual Father" and "The new hebdomadary Book," handwritten by her confessor, Michael Stephen Robinson IV, to commemorate her profession.[26]

CLARE JOSEPH DICKINSON

Accompanying Bernardina Matthews and her two nieces on their foundation voyage, was an Antwerp Carmelite chosen to replace Mary Margaret Brent. Despite the latter's death, Antwerp Carmel continued to play a very significant role in the foundation through the dedicated work of yet another Carmelite, Teresa Cowdrey, who was also not destined to journey to America. Without her, however, the American foundation might never have occurred. Through a close friend, Monsieur de Villegas d'Estainbourg, a member of the Grand Council of Brussels, Teresa Cowdrey collected most of the funds needed for the voyage and foundation.[27] The most likely choice of the Antwerp community for the foundation in America, she was bypassed for another sister, Clare Joseph Dickinson, whose talents were more appealing to the chaplain, Charles Neale, who had assumed the task of co-founder of Carmel in America.

Frances Dickinson was born July 12, 1755 in London, England. Very little is known about her background. George Dickinson was her father; Halford was her mother's family

From an early American painting of Clare Joseph Dickinson which hangs in 'Chandler's Hope'.

In their devotion to the Sacred Heart, the American Carmelites stand firmly within the more humanistic tradition of spirituality.

name.[28] She had brothers and at least one sister and was educated by the Ursulines in France.[29] When she entered the monastery of Antwerp on May 1, 1772, she brought a dowry of 100 pounds sterling. She was professed as Clare Joseph of the Sacred Heart on June 3, 1773 at the monastery of Antwerp.[30] By the time she left the Lowlands for Maryland, she was thirty-five years of age and had been a professed member of the "English Teresian monastery of Antwerp" for seventeen years.

Unlike the other members of the group who were returning to their families in Southern Maryland, she was the one missionary to a foreign land, the one who was probably never again to see either her family or her English friends. Apparently, she cherished friendship. Among her papers are letters written to her during the early years of her religious life by her spiritual director and by her close Jesuit friend, J. Spencer. One of Spencer's ends with poetry: "If some wandering traveller should stray... Be sure to nurse him and then all is right/With drams, with punch, with caffe [sic] and with tea/With sweet discourse, tis needless more to say - adieu. Yrs most sincerely and affec[tionat]ely till death, J. Spencer +" Just as telling and poignant is the list of the anniversaries of each of the nuns in Antwerp.[31]

CHARLES NEALE

The final member of the founding party, revered by the first generation of American Carmelites as a founder and father, was the Jesuit-trained chaplain of Antwerp Carmel, Charles Neale, who was related to each of the Maryland women connected with the foundation. Through his mother, Anne Brooke Neale, he shared with Bernardina a common ancestor in Dr. Thomas Matthews: Neale's great, great grandfather was Bernardina's great grandfather. Through his father, William Neale, he was closely related to Mary Margaret Brent. Furthermore, Charles' sister, Mary Neale, married Bernardina's brother, William Matthews, making their children, Sisters Eleanora and Aloysia, the nieces of both Charles and Bernardina.[32]

Just as the Maryland Catholic gentry were bound together by complex and multiple family ties, so were the founders of Carmel in America. One of the characteristics of the community they established in Port Tobacco was the bondedness created by multiple family ties, not only among the founders but also among the Maryland women who entered the community after its foundation in 1790.[33] These blood relationships, often considered hazardous in religious communities in the more recent past, probably stabilized the new community and contributed to its success, its sense of presence to the surrounding community and the early Church, and its determination and ability to survive.

Charles Neale's father, William, was born in Charles County into Maryland's aristocracy.[34] In 1725 he inherited a generous estate, "Chandler's Hope," from his wealthy uncle, William Chandler. It was here that Charles was born on October 10, 1751, the third of eleven children. It was here on the Neale family estate that the founders formally began Carmelite life in the United States. They lived at "Chandler's Hope" from July 21 to October 15, 1790. It was Charles' portion of "Chandler's Hope," moreover, that he traded with Baker Brooke for a property at Port Tobacco that was more suitable for a permanent monastery.[35]

Like his brothers, Charles was sent as a boy to school in the Low Countries where he received an education with the English Jesuits.[36] One of the six children of William and Anne Brooke Neale who joined religious life, he entered the Jesuits in 1771.[37] When the Society of Jesus was suppressed by Pope Gregory XIV in 1773, Charles was still a novice at Ghent. Although he was prevented from professing his vows, he was ordained and remained in Europe to minister as a priest.[38]

His initial connection with the Maryland project began

in 1780. With the consent of Father John Howard, last rector of the Jesuit College at Liege, Charles reluctantly accepted the pressing invitation of his cousin, Mary Margaret Brent, to become the confessor of the Antwerp community.[39] He was twenty-nine years old. During the next ten years of "in-service training" he was educated for what became his life project. He had four years to absorb Mary Margaret Brent's perception of Carmelite life along with her dreams and plans for the new foundation. During this period he also went at regular intervals to Hoogstraet as an occasional confessor thereby functioning as a communication link between the two prioresses and their hopes for the future of Carmelite life.[40]

SPIRITUALITY OF FOUNDERS

Now that the characters who took part in the Carmelite adventure are in place, questions do arise. Details of their long, difficult journey to America are available, but what can be known about their spiritual journey? What light does the journal of their forty day sea voyage throw on their personalities and their spirituality? What can be learned from the materials and supplies they brought with them from Europe to the new foundation? Even more importantly, how are these founders revealed to us in the documents, books and artifacts they left behind?

Bernardina Matthews and Mary Margaret Brent seemed to have had much in common. They shared a similar spirituality characteristic of British Catholics born and reared in Southern Maryland under the guidance of the Jesuits and educated in the recusant community of the Lowlands. They stand within the moderate humanistic French school as it was mediated to them through the English Jesuit inheritance and through central elements of Teresian/Carmelite spirituality.[41]

The openness to contemplative prayer seen in the nuns' writings is distinctly Carmelite in character and would have been encouraged and supported by the writings of Teresa which they possessed in English translation and which they brought to America. A poem written by Brent, although possessing little literary merit, nevertheless paraphrases the heart of the ancient Carmelite Rule with its emphasis on solitary prayer:

> A.Lone with God, a lone, now in your Cell
> Let all your thoughts, in recollection dwell
> for its the obligation, of your State
> Still on the law, of God, to meditate
> to keep Strict Silence and to watch in prayer.[42]

Brent's understanding of the centrality and meaning of solitary prayer for the Carmelite is developed clearly in other writings that suggest a possible familiarity with an early Carmelite text, *The Institution of The First Monks.* Certainly they show the unmistakable influence of Teresa's teachings for whom contemplative prayer, not simply meditation, is seen as the goal of the Carmelite.

> Others must seek god but you must find him. others must serve God but you must adhere to him[.] others must believe in god[,] know, love, & honour him, but you must taste, understand, know, & injoy him.[43]

> ...for w[he]n once his heart is thus habituated, he will find in it So Sweet a receptacle & Dwelling-place for God, th[a]t he will not know how to live without the peace, comfort, & Spiritual refection th[i]s brings with it[44]

Brent does not speak, as some of the Jesuit confessors do, of raising the mind to God but the heart. For her, affections of the heart, including human friendship, are conducive to spiritual growth, and contemplation is not only a goal but a profound love experience pervading her life, which she desires for all her daughters.[45]

My heart Seraphick wounded deep by love
Now raised to my heavenly Spouse above
Petitions him that Arrows all divine
May wound & burn my Childrens hearts like Mine...
and on this day make Each one know I will
and am their tender loveing Mother Still
their bossoms with my Spirrit blest to fill[46]

The dependence on the experience of Teresa of Avila to interpret her own experience is indisputable here.[47] What is also obvious is that while their Jesuit confessors wrote about prayer more often in the context of meditation and Ignatian spirituality, the Carmelites had their own characteristic perception and experience. These were not necessarily in opposition, especially in the case of the moderate humanistic school of the Lowland Jesuits. When their confessors were influenced by the more rigoristic continental French school, however, there were two different strands of spirituality operative in their lives. There is no evidence that these were conflictual for the Carmelites, but they were present.

In their devotion to the Sacred Heart, the American Carmelites stand firmly within the more humanistic tradition. It is easy to understand their openness and affinity to this Christological devotion. First of all, it had been taught by the Jesuits and practiced in the Maryland mission. Mary Brent and Anne Matthews probably grew into it as children and through it established the kind of identification with Jesus that made them desire and pursue Carmelite life. Secondly, in its emphasis on the humanity of Christ, on love and interiority, it provided a fertile soil for the teachings of Teresa (and also of Ignatius) for whom Jesus Christ is central. Thirdly, in its deepest meanings and development, devotion to the Sacred Heart as it became infused with Carmelite tradition opened into the experience of contemplative love.

This emphasis on love and experience is seen in so many of the founders' poems, not only Bernardina's and Mary Margaret Brent's, but Clare Joseph's from her early days in Antwerp. She writes in 1787:

> Within my heart D[ea]r Spouse you build a cell
> where Sweets are tasted w[hi]ch no tongue can tell
> where we with mutual love together meet
> with unrelented constancy & love.

Two years earlier Clare had written:

> My Dearest Spouses in My heart I bear,
> My Love for them has deeply fix'd 'em there;
> In this Sweet habitation Ever Dwell,
> Let it be Each ones Temple Each ones Cell...
> Let its Enflamed acts, yours Dignify,
> Its Burning flames, the fire you want Supply;[48]

Although the American Carmelites stressed the experience of God, theirs was a very practical, dignified, restrained piety with definite ecumenical overtones. While placing little emphasis on miracles and visions, it stressed interior dispositions and the acceptance of daily life and tasks in a spirit of love and availability to God's will. Grounded in a deep respect for the movement of the Holy Spirit in each person, which is basic to an understanding and experience of contemplative prayer, their spirituality correlated well with their inherited position of political liberty and the rights of conscience.[49] We see striking evidence of this in Brent's remarkable essays on "Regulations for Superiority" and "Explication of the 3 vows" written in 1781. For example, she writes:

> If they have anything to propose against her orders, she should hear them with patience, and if possible often approve their reasons... [and] say D[ea]r Sister you reasons are very good - I do not dislike what you propose, but for the present my D[ea]r Child, let it be

> don as I say -and offer up to God your difficultys in it... She ought to use the same moderation and sweetness - and only seek the amendment of the faults and not the confusion of the delinquent -never to reprehend in moments of passion, or with a mind and voice agitated, nor any terms that can exasperate the party...[50]

The language Brent employes in her reflection on being a superior reveals a respect for personal conscience and a deep recognition of the role of persuasion and rational discourse. In her abhorrence of coercion and hardness, she portrays an uncommon gentility, humility and mutual respect that speak not only of a spirituality akin to both Francis de Sales and Teresa of Avila but also of her upbringing among the Catholic gentry of British America.

The Maryland gentry carried in their collective soul the memory of a colony founded on the principles of religious toleration and mutual respect. Just as deep, however, was the later memory of disenfranchisement, deprivation of religious liberty and exclusion from public service effected by the penal laws. Even though Maryland Catholics did not suffer the loss of their wealth or social position, they did suffer the disgrace of second-class citizenship. Liberty of conscience was a crucial value in shaping their self-understanding and their relationship with God and others, just as it was for the English Teresians for somewhat different reasons.[51]

A question arises here concerning Clare Joseph and Charles Neale. How similar to the two older American Carmelites were they in their orientation and spirituality? This is an important question because these two, together, had an enormous influence on the development of the new foundation. They lived in close proximity to each other for thirty-three years. Their friendship and collaboration were the bedrock on which the new Carmel grew. After Bernardina's death May 11, 1800, Clare Joseph was named prioress by John Carroll and remained in office by later elections until her own death March 27, 1830. Neale was the spiritual director of the community until his death in 1823.

Clare Joseph certainly experienced in Antwerp the traditions seen in the two older American women.[52] While her papers must be studied thoroughly from the perspective of Carmelite tradition and contemplative prayer, there is no doubt that she transmitted to the American Carmelites she trained and led the positive value of freedom of conscience. She seemed to want to reinforce it, in fact, in her last illness in a note to one of the sisters:

> My Dear Child as to your private papers concerning your conscience and any spiritual advice or instruction which your confessor may give[,] The Superior has no liberty or power to look at or read...she is not to read either the one which you write nor the answer which you receive...

And in a memo six months earlier, she wrote:

> According to the opi=nion of the ancient Superiors of our Mother house of Antwerp, no Prioress pos=sesses the Power or privi=lege of inspecting or peru=sing the Confessions or Private Conscience Papers of the Living or deceased Religious; nor the Private letters She may have given them leave to write...[53]

In trying to understand what traditions were operative in Clare Joseph's spirituality, one detail deserves attention here. Her contemporaries in Port Tobacco believed Clare Joseph had helped to compile the *Pious Guide To Prayer and Devotion* published in 1792 by the Jesuits at Georgetown and designed in part to refute the Jansenist criticism of the Sacred Heart devotion. Although the Jesuits, themselves, have no record of her collaboration, the oral tradition of the Baltimore Carmelites has passed on this belief. If she did help Charles Neale and the early Jesuits in this task, real light is thrown on her place along the spectrum of eighteenth century spirituality.[54]

Charles Neale was, like his cousins Mary Brent and Bernardina Matthews, a child of the Maryland gentry educated by the Jesuits of the Lowlands. It is known that "Jesuit training at St. Omers, Liege and Bruges, in the mid-eighteenth century, emphasized devotion to the Sacred Heart," and fell within the more humanistic tradition.[55] Nevertheless, during the long years of education and ministry in the Lowlands, he had also incorporated into his spirituality some of the influences of a more rigoristic tradition.

Historians of spirituality see in Charles Neale and Clare Joseph this leaning toward the more rigorous emphasis found in continental French spirituality with its stress on obedience to the rule, the superior and regularity of life. Here God's will is mediated more through the superior and the rule than through inner dispositions. In fact, interior movements of the passions, emotions and will are suspect, while rational control exercised by the intellect is encouraged.

This is reflected, Joseph Chinnici believes, not only in Charles Neale's papers but also in extant letters of spiritual direction belonging to Clare from her Antwerp days. It is seen in her reflections on religious profession, spirituality and community life at Port Tobacco. The fact that she was a boarding student at the Ursulines in Paris during her formative years might account for some of the influences found in her writings that differ from the American Carmelites. The difference is certainly reflected in considerations on the vows, attitudes toward the rule and the role of the superior, and on the approach to meditation relative to contemplation. Chinnici suggests it is even seen in comparing devotion to the Sacred Heart in Clare Joseph and M.M. Brent.

On the other hand, the journal describing the 1790 voyage is written in Clare Joseph's hand and unquestionably reveals facets of her personality and spirituality, even if the daily account was a project to which all six of the travellers contributed. The journal is impressive both for its honesty and its lack of drama in the face of very difficult physical and psychological conditions. Clare Joseph does not spiritualize the nuns' experience of the Captain's behavior, character or lack of refinement. Neither does she hide the attitudes of condescension and disgust with which she and her cultured and educated companions looked upon the captain and the other passengers.[56]

Clare Joseph's keen and lively sense of humor draws a picture and creates a mood that can conceal the seriousness of the hardships endured. The nuns' fear of perishing from storms and from hunger is evident, however, in the promises they made on May 7, May 22 and June 6 "to perform at our leisure when settled" certain devotions and prayers.[57] They were not above bargaining with God for their lives and their new foundation, nor believing that prayer and promises could change the direction of divine providence.

The journal reveals an overwhelming sense of God's providence. God's intervention is really experienced in ordinary events, like the calming of the sea. The influence of Ignatian spirituality is evident in this as well as in the desire for frequent communion, a yearning by no means universally cultivated at the end of the eighteenth century and definitely frowned on by the Jansenists and the more rigorous side of French spirituality. Teresa of Avila wrote of such a longing for communion, and Carmelites have always echoed her desire. How important a place frequent communion held in the lives and spirituality of the entire group is evident from Clare Joseph's careful detail of the Mass, the reception of communion and the part played by the priest, Charles Neale.[58]

While Bernardina and her nieces are real but shadowy figures in the journal, Neale's portrait is sketched very clearly. A certain rigorous side of his personality, apparent even on the trip, is balanced by a concrete ability to care for the seasick nuns with genuine humor and concern. The determination to sacrifice even his food for them on board ship indicates a depth of involvement that will eventually motivate him to purchase with his own patrimony the property for their monastery in Port Tobacco. While there are faint hints of the inflexibility that is mentioned as early as 1780 by John Howard, rector of the English College at Bruges, and much later by John Carroll in Maryland, apparently Clare Joseph and the other Carmelites were accustomed to tease him about his sternness. While he exercised a strong authority in the group, he was deeply loved and he was accepted in his role.

It remains difficult even today to analyze Neale's lifelong ministry to the nuns or the motivation that prompted it. Not even his superiors could persuade him to leave Mount Carmel to fill the leadership roles assigned to him when the Society was reestablished and he made his first vows as a Jesuit on August 18, 1805. Neither could these superiors persuade the nuns to let him go.[59]

He was not an outsider helping the community. He shared deeply in their everyday life, gave retreats and conferences, wrote poems for community celebrations, handled numerous business details and managed the farm and slaves through which the nuns supported themselves. There can be no doubt that his spirituality was formative for Carmel and yet Carmel had to be formative for him, also.[60] That Neale was to blame, as John Carroll suggests, for the nuns' refusal to teach in 1793 is questionable.[61] Evidence suggests that there was a strong enough tradition operative among the English Teresians of Hoogstraet and Antwerp to make them quite capable of such a decision on their own.[62]

LIFE AND CULTURE OF AMERICAN CARMELITES

From the beginning of the American foundation, a level of culture and intellectual life, characteristic of both the Maryland gentry and the English Teresians, was encouraged. Over one thousand books, many inscribed "Monastery of the English Carmelites of Antwerp," were transported to Maryland, presumably by Clare Joseph and Charles Neale on the ship called "Brothers." Conscious of planting both the ancient tradition of Carmel and religious life for women in the newborn nation, the founders brought a board, eclectic theological library, historical records on the Antwerp and Lowland Carmels, and numerous materials on spirituality, prayer and Carmelite life. These embodied all the currents and traditions that would form and grow into American Carmelite life.

Within this framework, life was poor and simple for the daughters of the Maryland gentry who joined the founders at the end of the eighteenth century. Clare Joseph opens a window on the ordinary life of everyday in "A Song expressive of my Cordial Thanks and Praise of my Nuns admirable Ingenuity" written in 1811. This excerpt begins with the third stanza:

In Carving they Excell,
In Drawing Painting too,
Each of us here can tell,
How Justly Praise is Due;
They Card they Knit and Spin,
Well Versed in holy Prayer,
Can Use the Cotton Gin,
And of their Souls take care.

They Weave both wool and thread,
To Cloath (sic) the White and Black,
They make the finest Bread,
Of this they have the Knack;
In all they Strive to yield,

True Glory to their Spouse,
And in Fair Virtues Field,
They walk and keep their Vows.

The Pen and Needle too,
Perform their Clever Part,
With Pleasure all I View,
As Flowing from the Heart;
For you my Children Dear,
My Feeble Voice I'll raise,
That Jesus May Draw Near,
And fill with Joy your Days.

Now here my Leave I take,
And bid you All farewell
Eat up your little Cake,
In Love of God Excell...[63]

In spite of the limitations of Clare Joseph's poetry, there is no other single document from Port Tobacco days that sheds more light on the nuns' daily occupations and abilities. Their contemplative life was lived then, as it had been lived for generations, in small communities in the midst of very ordinary, human tasks, experiences and relationships.

Two centuries have passed since Bernardina Matthews, Eleanora and Aloysia Matthews, Clare Joseph Dickinson and Charles Neale stepped off the sloop at Brent's Landing, with all their baggage and all their hopes, to live out the charism of prayer on American soil in service of God's people. The beauty of the life they began lives on today in their spiritual descendants. It will live on into the future because of the human need and desire for God.

NOTES

1. There were two priests who made the journey with the nuns. English-born Robert Plunkett, who had left the Jesuits even before the Suppression of the Society in 1773, had secured permission from Propaganda Fide to go to America as a missionary. He simply travelled with the party. Although he became the first president of Georgetown University, he served in that capacity for less than two years. He had volunteered for the American mission because of its pastoral, not its educational needs. See the forthcoming history of Georgetown University by Robert Emmett Curran, S.J.

2. The Carmelite Rule was written sometime between 1206 and 1214 by Albert of Vercelli, the Patriarch of Jerusalem. Although he was most certainly setting down a way of life already lived for some time by western hermits on Mount Carmel, it is only in the thirteenth century that indisputable evidence of their presence there exists.

3. See Joachim Smet, O.Carm., *The Carmelites, A History of the Brothers of Our Lady of Mount Carmel,* vol. 1 (Rome: Carmelite Institute, 1975); Elias Friedman, O.C.D., *The Hermits of Mount Carmel, A Study in Carmelite Origins* (Rome: Teresianum, 1979); Carlo Cicconetti, O.Carm., *The Rule of Carmel* (Darien, Illinois: Carmelite Spiritual Center, 1984).

4. This gradual affiliation over two centuries is detailed by Joachim Smet in *Cloistered Carmel* (Rome: Institutum Carmelitanum, 1986) and in Smet, *The Carmelites*, vol. 1, pp. 103-116.

5. Today there are two Carmelite Orders: the Carmelites of the Ancient Observance and the Discalced Carmelites.

6. While Anne Worsley came from the Mechlin monastery and had been trained by both Anne of Jesus (Brussels monastery) and Anne of St. Bartholomew (Spanish-Antwerp monastery), Margaret Baston and Anne Duynes came from Brussels, Clare Laithwaite from Louvain and Teresa Ward from Mons. Teresa Ward, who dressed as a man to leave England, was the sister of the indomitable Mary Ward (1585-1645) who founded in 1609 the first community of unenclosed women religious, the Institute of the Blessed Virgin Mary.

7. For example, Rose Fisher, St. John Fisher's grand-niece was professed in Antwerp in 1636 and Lady Anne Somerset, "daughter of the most illustrious Henry Earl Marquess of Worcester of the royal family of Plantagenet" in 1643. Although Anne Worsley's paternal great grandfather, Sir James Worsley, was a page of Henry VIII, Keeper of Lions in the Tower, Groom of Robes and Governor of the Island of Wight, her father disobeyed Queen Elizabeth's order in 1560 to return to England and therefore lost all property under the recusancy laws. Her maternal great grandfather, Sir Nicholas Hervey, a Gentleman of the Privy Chamber to Henry VIII, was present with Thomas More at Andres in 1520. During Elizabeth's reign, Anne's grandfather, Thomas Hervey, went abroad to Spain and then to the Spanish Netherlands because of his religion. See Anne Hardman, SND, *English Carmelites in Penal Times* (London: Burns Oates and Washbourne, 1936), pp. 79-80, 59-60, 136-40.

8. The first native of Maryland to become a nun was Mary Digges who was a canoness regular of the Holy Sepulchre at Liege as early as 1721. She was Mary Margaret Brent's aunt. See Brent letter to "My dearest Cousin" (Charles Neale or one of his two priest brothers) written around 1776: "I suppose you have heard of Aunt Mary Digges death, long ago." See Archives of the Carmelite Monastery of Baltimore, Maryland (hereafter cited as ACMB), II, 2.

9. See James Hennesey, S.J., "Several Youths Sent From Here: Native-Born Priests and Religious of English America, 1634-1776," in Nelson H. Minnich et al, ed., *Studies in Catholic History in Honor of John Tracy Ellis* (Wilmington, Delaware: Michael Glazier, 1985), pp. 1-26. Two things should be noted: Eleanor Wharton was Mary Margaret Brent's aunt. Her brother, Robert, was married to a woman who was also named Anna Maria Parnham. See letter of Brent concerning her aunt in Lierre in ACMB, II, 2, or Charles Warren Currier, *Carmel in America* (Darien, Illinois: Carmelite Press, 1989), p. 386. (A bicentennial reprint of the 1890 history.)

10. Antwerp Carmel, because of the long term leadership of Anne of the Ascension (1619-44), had the influence of a motherhouse for the English and Dutch houses founded from it. Hoogstraet, however, had its own distinctive life and characteristics. It was founded in 1678 under the patronage of the Lady Rheingrave, Maria Gabriela de la Laing, Duchess of Hoogstraet, whose family exercised certain rights and duties and considerable influence in the life of the community during its one hundred sixteen years in the Flemish Lowlands. Every new member, before entering Carmel, was received at the Rheingrave

Castle and frequently given her religious name by the Duchess. The family, moreover, played a central role in liturgical ceremonies and religious celebrations at the monastery. When the War of Succession broke out in 1701, the community, under the leadership of Mother Mary Teresa, Lady Rheingrave's daughter, was moved for its safety to the Rheingrave Castle in Mechlin. It was eleven years before they returned from this exile to the Hoogstraet monastery.

11. Mary Brent's grandfather, Jesse Wharton, was acting Governor of Maryland in 1676 when Charles Calvert, Lord Baltimore, returned to England. Her grandmother, Elizabeth Sewall, was the daughter of Jane Lowe and Secretary Henry Sewall, a stepson of the third Lord Baltimore.

12. Giles claimed extensive Maryland land because of his marriage to the daughter of the King of the Piscataway Indians. Giles was a man of prominence in Maryland from its earliest founding. When Governor Leonard Calvert returned to England in 1643, he appointed Giles Brent Deputy Governor in his absence. See Chester Horton Brent, *The Descendants of Colonel Giles Brent, Capt. George Brent and Robert Brent, Gentleman* (Rutland, Vermont: Tuttle Publishing Company, 1946), p. 52.

13. Ibid., pp. 43-50. Margaret Brent was not given a vote.

14. Unfortunately, there is no source to substantiate the claim made by Anne Hardman that Mary Brent first crossed the ocean as a child to attend a convent school in the Lowlands. Following the Glorious Revolution in 1689, the Maryland Catholic gentry were prevented by penal laws from providing education in their faith for their children. They, therefore, sent their children to be educated in the English colleges of the Low Countries. Whereas there are many records verifying the education of sons in Europe, there is little evidence that daughters were regularly sent. Eleanor Darnell and her sister seemed to have received an education in the Lowlands. When most young women left home for Europe, however, as thirty-three did between 1721 and 1776, it was to join religious orders. See Hardman, p. 106; Robert Emmett Curran, S.J., *American Jesuit Spirituality, The Maryland Tradition, 1634-1900* (New York: Paulist Press, 1988), pp. 12-13; Thomas W. Spalding, *The Premier See, A History of the Archdiocese of Baltimore, 1789-1989* (Baltimore: The Johns Hopkins University Press, 1989), pp. 1-5, and "Natives of Maryland in Religious Houses and Seminaries Abroad from 1684 to 1788," in Edwin W. Beitzell, *The*

Jesuit Missions of St. Mary's County, Maryland (Abell, Maryland, 1976), pp. 313-321; Thomas Hughes, S.J., "Educational Convoys to Europe in the Olden Time," *American Ecclesiastical Review* 29 (1903); Hennesey, pp. 1-26).

15. ACMB, II, 2, the Antwerp Carmelites to other monasteries of the Order. This is undoubtedly an account of the life of M.M. Brent written by the Antwerp Carmelites at the time of her death. Manuscript is preserved in the Carmelite Monastery at Ghent. Copy made by Rev. P. Corballis, OSB, in 1928. The punctuation, spelling and capitalization are given as they appear in the original.

16. See Horton Brent, p. 103. In his will he left "daughter Mary in convent at Antwerp 100 pounds."

17. ACMB, II, 2, Antwerp Carmel to Carmelite monasteries, account of her life.

18. Her confirmation before her profession seems to corroborate the doubts raised about her previous education in a convent in the Low Countries. It seems likely she would have been confirmed during her school days had she been in Europe.

19. Besides being an attorney at Law, Thomas Matthews had been trained in medicine. To save Jesuit lands from confiscation by Lord Baltimore, Father Thomas Copley, S.J. transferred to Matthews his own landrights for St. Thomas Manor by means of a personal trust. From 1649 until 1662, therefore, St. Thomas Manor, acquired under "Conditions of Plantation" was held by Thomas Matthews Esq. as trustee for the Society of Jesus. For returning the property to the Jesuits, Matthews was later recognized by the General of the Jesuits in a commendation dated in Rome, February 9, 1900: "Your Reverence will not forget to entertain a deep sense of gratitude to the Matthews family, and not only to entertain but show that gratitude: and this not merely on your own part but in the name of the whole Society; for the Fidelity to trust on the part of the first member of that family, is both very rare and beyond price..." Found in Magdalen M. Machall, *Our Colonial Ancestors* (Private Manuscript, 1963) at the Maryland Historical Society. See also Edwin Warfield Beitzell, *The Jesuit Missions of St. Mary's County, Maryland,* 1960, pp. 9, 23-27.

20. See Harry Wright Newman, *The Maryland Semmes and Kindred Families* (Maryland Historical Society, 1956), pp. 236-39, 243-44; Lois Greene Carr, "Notable American Women" in Edward T. James, ed., *A Biographical Dictionary,* vol. 1 (Cambridge, Mass.: Belkrap Press, 1971), pp. 509-10.

21. See Newman, pp. 244-45.

22. Currier, p. 56.

23. Before leaving Belgium, Mother Bernardina had a strong premonition of his death. She had said to the community that she would never see him again.

24. See ACMB, III, 2. While the Profession Records of Chichester Carmel (formerly in Hoogstraet) record September 30, 1755 as the date of Bernardina's profession, there is a hebdomadary book handwritten by her confessor giving the following dates: Clothing-September 30, 1754, Profession-November 24, 1755, Veiling-December 3, 1755. Such discrepancies are difficult to explain and to resolve. Ann Hill received the habit and was professed as Ann Lewis (or Louisa) Teresa Joseph of Our Blessed Lady at the same time as Mother Bernardina.

25. Archives of the Archdiocese of Baltimore; for copy see Currier, pp. 73-4.

26. ACMB, III, 2. The leather-bound hebdomadary book is written in beautiful calligraphy. It was a present meant to last for a lifetime.

27. Balthassar Joseph Ignace de Villegas d'Estainbourg was the chief benefactor of the Maryland foundation and was sometimes called a founder. He continued to send money even after the monastery was established. Although he intended that 22,000 florins should go to the community after his death and the death of his cousin, his heirs successfully contested the will.

When Joseph II issued an edict in 1782 closing the monasteries of the Netherlands, de Villegas worked with Madame Louise of France, aunt of Louis XVI and a Carmelite at St. Denis in Paris, to transfer communities of religious women to French monasteries. He was given a portrait of the Princess, Sister Teresa of St. Augustine, which is still in the possession of the Baltimore Carmelites.

28. Because the Antwerp community lost many of its records when the nuns fled to England in 1794 following the invasion of the French, there is very little information available concerning Clare Joseph's background and family. Some facts are found in correspondence from Sr. Teresa Cowdrey, who writes from Lanherne Carmel (formerly Antwerp) after its resettlement. Cowdrey, Clare's childhood friend, mentions Clare's Uncle Halford who lives in Yorkshire and his

married daughter, Nancy (Halford), in Oxford. There is a Father John Halford, born in London August 5, 1753 of Thomas H. Halford and Ann Welch (or Walsh). John was a priest educated at St. Omers who "went to the mission" in England and served 17 years at Torre Abbey in the district of Tormoham, in the county of Devon. The fact that, during the foundation journey along the coast of England, Dickinson mentions sending a letter to Torre Abbey supports the assumption John Halford may have been a cousin.

29. In ACMB is a book belonging to Mother Clare Joseph: *Formulaire de Prieres Chretiennes Pour Passer Saintement La Journee.* It was written for the use of the young ladies in the boarding schools conducted by the Ursulines. It is inscribed with these words: "This was the prayer book of our dear Rev. Mother Clare Joseph while a pensioner at the Ursuline Convent." An addition in pencil reads: "Paris - France."

30. The amount of her dowry is gained through transfer documents at the time of her departure from Antwerp when she was given the dowry as part of the community's estate in the new world. A document dated Antwerp, April the 12th, 1790 reads: "For my separating from the English Carmelites of Antwerp to go to found in America, I acknowledge to have received from the Superior & Community of the said Convent the sum of one hundred pounds sterling, all due in payment for the same sum given at my profession in the year 1773. Witness my hand Clare Joseph of the Sacred Heart of Jesus. Alias, Frances Dickinson." ACMB, III, 3. See also ACMB, II, 3, from Lanherne Carmel to Baltimore Carmel, February 20, 1928.

31. ACMB, II, 1; III, 3.

32. Charles Neale's grandparents were Mary Brent and Roswell Neale. Mary Brent Neale was the sister of Mother Mary Margaret Brent's grandfather, Robert Brent, and therefore her great aunt.

Dr. Thomas Matthews was married twice. Charles Neale was descended from his first wife, Bernardina Matthews from his second. This means Dr. Thomas Matthews was both great, great grandfather, through their father, and great, great, great grandfather, through their mother, to the two Matthews nieces.

33. By way of example, we see that through Charles Neale's mother, Anne Brooke, he and his nieces were related to the Boarmans. His grandmother, Ann Boarman, was the daughter of Major William Boarman (1630-1709), the progenitor of the Boarman family in Maryland who came to the colony about 1645. Two Boarmans, Matilda and Elizabeth, entered the community in 1799 and Mary Bradford, whose mother was a Boarman, in 1802. Mary Ann Mudd was also related to the Boarmans. Moreover, a great uncle of Charles and Bernardina married Mary Jane Mudd, daughter of Captain

James Mudd.

34. By 1642, the progenitor of the Neale family, Captain James Neale, was in Maryland with full manorial rights to 2,000 acres he named "Wollaston." He had maintained an important position in the court of King Charles I and Queen Henrietta Maria and did not settle permanently in the colony until around 1660 when he returned with his wife, Anne Gill, and their four children. James Neale was Charles' great, great grandfather.

35. See ACMB, III, 1, for the original land grant for Chandler's Hope, dated 1674, given by Cecil Calvert and signed by Charles Calvert. Charles Neale inherited his portion of the family estate in 1784 when his brother Raphael died. Because Charles was a priest, his father did not bequeath property to him.

The monastery at Port Tobacco, purchased with Charles Neale's patrimony, was dedicated October 15, 1790 to the Sacred Hearts of Jesus, Mary and Joseph. The community lived there for forty-one years. In 1831 they moved to Aisquith Street, Baltimore City, and in 1873 to a newly built monastery on Biddle Street in Baltimore. In 1961 the community moved again to a new monastery in Dulaney Valley, Baltimore County.

36. See ACMB, III, 4, for a biography of Charles Neale by Benedict Fenwick, S.J., who assisted him on his deathbed. Fenwick believes Charles went to the Jesuit College in Bruge when he was ten years old. The emigre English Jesuit College at St. Omers was transferred first to Bruge in 1762 and later to Liege following the suppression of the Jesuits in 1773.

37. Joseph died at St. Omers after making vows of devotion as a Jesuit on his deathbed, Anne was a Poor Clare in Aire, France, and four were Jesuits. While the oldest, William, died in a Manchester asylum after serving in Lancashire, the other two Jesuits, Leonard and Francis, played prominent roles in the lives of the Carmelites in Port Tobacco, in the restoration of the Society of Jesus, and in the American Church under John Carroll's leadership. Leonard was second Archbishop of Baltimore.

38. See ACMB, III, 4, for "A play composed and written out by Rev. Charles Neale, S.J. Acted by the Students at the College of Liege." In 1789-90 he was probably in Liege.

39. See ACMB, III, 3 and III, 4, for letters of Howard and Neale. See also Currier, pp. 387-88; Currier has a mistake in the Howard letter. In the original the Neale mentioned is clearly Leonard, not Charles.

40. Jesuit confessors were not unusual in the English-speaking Carmels. Anne of Jesus had fought against Nicholas Doria, Vicar General of the Teresian Carmelites, for freedom for the nuns to choose their own confessors, as Teresa of Avila had directed in her Constitutions. Anne of the Ascension was equally possessive of this right. Benedict Zimmerman, OCD, says: "In the Low Countries, the English convents came entirely under the management of the Jesuits. This is easily explained[.] When there were English Discalced Carmelites at Antwerp, as happened from time to time, these, of course, did not fail to help the convent... But very often there were none, whereas there were always English Jesuits, and these made themselves so indispensable to the nuns that someone even left the latter a legacy [6000 florins from Mr. Erbery] that they might always secure the services of Jesuits, or after the suppression by the Holy See, of ex-Jesuits. [History shows] what great help they were, but still it was not exactly what St. Teresa intended." (Hardman, p. viii)

The Jesuit influence in the English Carmels was profound. Many of the nuns' relatives and friends were Jesuits and these Jesuits worked both in the Low Countries and in England during the persecutions. They ministered in disguise, they were imprisoned, they often escaped, but they were also put to death. "All through the years of persecution, the English Carmels were in close touch with Catholic affairs in England and their annals often contain references to the sufferings and death of the English martyrs."

41. See Curran, pp. 12-18; Joseph P. Chinnici, OFM, *Living Stones, The History and Structure of Catholic Spiritual Life in the United States* (New York: Macmillan Publishing Company, 1989), pp. 5-34. I am indebted to Joseph Chinnici for sharing by telephone some of the conclusions he has reached from researching the papers of the Carmelite founders and Charles Neale in the Archives of the Carmelite Monastery in Baltimore. He will present his findings at the Carmelite Bicentennial Symposium at Loyola College, August, 1990. I draw and build on his analysis in the material which follows.

It should be noted here that John Carroll was also influenced in his spirituality by the moderate humanistic French school.

42. ACMB, II, 2, 6. The punctuation, spelling and abbreviations in this text, and those which follow, are given as they appear in the

original. Chapter 8 of the Carmelite Rule reads: "Each one of you is to stay in his own cell or nearby, pondering the Lord's law day and night and keeping watch at his prayers unless attending to some other duty."

43. Ibid., a fragment on examen of conscience.

44. Ibid., a fragment on raising heart to God.

45. This is not meant to imply that the Jesuit confessors never encouraged this approach. There is, for example, a significant letter of spiritual direction from Edward Baptist Newton on the love of God. See ACMB, II, 1.

46. Ibid.

47. See Kiernan Kavanaugh and Otilio Rodriguez, *The Complete Works of St. Teresa of Avila,* vol. 1 (Washington, D.C.: Institute of Carmelite Studies, 1976) pp. 193-94. The symbolism of this poem suggests an obvious allusion to an experience of St. Teresa called by Carmelites the transpiercing or transverberation of her heart.

48. ACMB, III, 3.

49. I am indebted to Joseph Chinnici for much of this analysis.

50. ACMB, II, 2.

51. Freedom of conscience was a value for the English Teresians for two reasons. Firstly, English Catholics had lived through long years of persecution in their homeland. Many Catholics in the Low Countries had forfeited property and wealth in England in order to practice their religion freely. Secondly, following the lead of Anne of Jesus (Lobera), Anne of the Ascension (Worsley) had struggled for the freedom to follow the Constitutions of Alcala, which she considered St. Theresa's Constitutions for the nuns, rather than a later version approved for the Order. The Alcala Constitutions guaranteed the right of the nuns to choose their own confessors and Anne of the Ascension held on to this freedom for the English Teresians. Rather than change the Constitutions, she moved the Antwerp monastery from the jurisdiction of the Order to that of the Bishop of Antwerp. See notes, nos. 7 and 40.

52. Since Clare Joseph and Charles Neale were the ones from Antwerp Carmel, they must have had a role in bringing Brent's papers to Maryland and preserving them for posterity, unless Mother Bernardina, herself, asked that these be brought.

53. ACMB, III, 3, 52, December 31, 1829, Clare Joseph to one of the sisters three months before the former's death. End line hyphenation is indicated in text (=).

54. See Chinnici, p. 31; Curran, pp. 18-20, 151-161. Curran says that the Jansenists especially attacked the Sacred Heart devotion for the benevolent cast of its anthropology and soteriology. He adds: "In general there is a democratic thrust to the spirituality of the **Guide...** It presupposes a Catholic laity controlling its own devotional life. As Joseph Chinnici has pointed out, it is very much within the humanistic tradition of piety, Christocentric and optimistic in its encouragement of individuals to pursue piety interiorly with relatively little reliance on intermediaries or official structures."

55. Chinnici, p. 30. Father Thomas Lawson, a former Jesuit and active apostle of the Sacred Heart devotion, published *The Devotion to the Sacred Heart* in 1765. He was rector of the College of Bruge from 1766-69 when Charles Neale was most likely a student there. A copy of Lawson's book, belonging to Mary Margaret Brent and inscribed from her "cousin, Ignatius Francis Neale," is in the Baltimore Archives. See ACMB, X, 2, 118, for letters of John Corbett, S.J., to Prioress, 1927.

56. That honesty and straightforwardness were basic to Clare Joseph's personality is demonstrated in later correspondence from the Lanherne (Antwerp) Carmelites. In 1821 Mother Teresa de Tholozan, the prioress, and Sister Mary Joseph of the Martyrs write to clear up a misunderstanding with Clare Joseph. Clare had apparently written a strong, candid letter complaining of Sister Mary Joseph's correction of Clare's "free manner of writing." In a profuse apology, claiming the community had never "conceived the least shadow of offense by any of your most welcome letters," the Lanherne nuns assure Clare that "was it not for the great good you have done in the new World [we] should deeply regret your ever having left us." ACMB, II, 3.

57. See ACMB, III, 3, for document written by Clare Joseph, probably after the arrival in Maryland, which details the obligations incurred by the promises made at sea. See also Currier, p. 425.

58. The sacred vessels and altar stone used on board the ship are in the possession of the Baltimore Carmelites. The altar stone, used by "the glorious martyrs" in the tower of London, was brought by Sister Catherine Tunstal from England to Hoogstraet Carmel when she joined the community.

59. See ACMB, III, 5, or Currier, pp. 109-112, for correspondence between Clare Joseph Dickinson, Bishop John Carroll and Robert Molyneux, S.J., the Jesuit superior, regarding the latter's unsuccessful decision to appoint Neale the first novice master. In a letter dated October 1, 1806, Molyneux does appoint Neale vice-superior "over all Jesuits in Charles and St. Mary's Counties." Neale was one of the five ex-Jesuits who revived the Society in 1805. He made his final profession as a Jesuit at Georgetown November 13, 1806. "Twice he was superior of the Maryland Mission (1808-1811, 1821-1823) and once vice-superior (1817). As head of the mission he was a staunch, if not always diplomatic defender of the Society's jurisdictional prerogatives and property rights, especially in the controversy with Archbishop Ambrose Marechal over the Society's estates in Maryland. In 1823 through a concordant with William Dubourg, the Bishop of Louisiana, he initiated the Missouri Mission." (From notes of Robert Emmett Curran)

60. See note no. 41.

61. There is sufficient evidence to believe that Neale could be stubborn and intractable. His letters to Carroll and Marechal are sometimes blunt, harsh and ungracious in style and the Jesuit General blames him for imprudence. He was severely criticized for refusing to surrender the Jesuit properties to Archbishop Marechal.

62. See note nos. 7 and 40.

63. ACMB, III, 3, 23.

Brent

Matthews

Neale

The Journal of a Trip to America

EDITORIAL PROCEDURES

The goal of this bicentennial edition of Clare Joseph Dickinson's diary is a critical text which follows the original as closely as possible. No attempt is made to correct the original spelling except in cases of obvious ambiguity. The syntax, punctuation and spelling of the original manuscript are retained except for completing some consistent abbreviations, replacing the colonial thorn (y) with th, and inserting within brackets [ ] some necessary punctuation and clarification. The text frequently lacks terminal punctuation and capital letters at the beginning of sentences. Where there is an apparent end of a sentence, an extra space is inserted before the next sentence even when the first word of the new sentence does not begin with a capital letter. Interlineations are incorporated into the text and indicated by ↑↓. An illegible letter is indicated by a dot in angle brackets < . >; an illegible word by a dash < - >. The author's use of two lines (=) to denote end of the line hyphenation is retained regardless of its placement in the transcription. Material crossed out by the author is indicated in the end notes.

A.M.D.G.

Ontvangen van de Heer Chr. Neale

de Somma van Honderd en Twintig Guinees of à f 11„11—

Dertien Honderd Ses en Taggentig Guldens Hollandsche

voor de Passagie en Provisie (uitgenoomen de Wyn) in de

Cajuit van het Engels Fregat Schip Brothers Capt.

Alexand. Mc Dougall van Hier na New York

voor gemelde Heer Chr. Neale — en zyn geselschap

bestaande in het geheel in twee heeren en Vier Dames

Zullende de Capitein verpligt zyn dit geselschap van alle

het noodige zoo als het aan een Cajuit Tafel gebruyk„

lyk is te voorzien, en all het mogelyke gemaak en

bekwaamheid toe brengen.

Amsterdam den 23 April 1790

Herm. Hend. Damen

Passenger Receipts for passage on the Ship "Brothers".

7th A Calm upon the Coast of Nor=mandy. the Sick much better, they made an apple pye rather of ye Conventual Kind, wch how=ever Might have been pretty good, had the black cook Known how to have baked it Enough. but it Came on ye table with the paste half Dow & ye apples half raw. mr plun: at the expence of a deal of trouble made us a good pot of Coffee. & mr neale as usual Kind Enough to give us up his Share miss Mathews merrily drank our healths in a glass of gin grog wch Seem'd to go down pretty Sweetly for want of Something better... We Call'd for Eggs for our Supper & after waiting for em about 2 hours & a half; we fetch'd em with very keen appetites. Dividing an Egg between 2. wch by the by was more than good mr neale got the night before, for he Came of wth only about a quarter of one to his Share, (& glad was he to accept of a piece of bacon we had hid for him in a corner of a dirty hankerchief.) we were remarkeably merry over our Eggs when behold our mirth damp'd all on a sudden by means of a silly woman who came to us with a tail of a tub, frighted out of her senses, telling us we were in danger of perishing, wch news made us fall to our prayers & promises. but it happen'd to prove a false alarm & to our great Joy we were assur'd there had been no danger at all.

N. B. we had each of us 3 Eggs a piece except miss nelly & myself who had 2 apiece & divided ye 8th

8th fair wind & weather. a fishing boat came on board, ye Captain bought 4 cods some mackerel fresh herrings & a fine Scate. we had a very scanty dinner of it & mr neale took care to tell ye Captain in plain terms at public table yt we had not Enough, yt he expected

more .. ye open, but Just complain[t]
hints ye Captain, he made Some
hobling excuse Saying ye Cook
was Sick, but assured m^r neele
y^t he would give him a royal
Supper. We were all well to day
m^r matthews excepted who was
rather indisposed. Jervols alive to town abbey.

9th this morning we pass'd by ouxant
with a fair breeze & fine weather
Cross'd the mouth of y^e bay biscay
Enter'd into the atlantic ocean
on our way to Spain, going 8 or 9
mile an hour. a Scanty fish dinner
tho' a Sunday. we expect Some bacon
& Eggs for Supper, but very likely
Shall be disappointed. y^e Captain to
make amends we supose for his Stingi
=ness at dinner, treated us in y^e afternoon
with a glass of madera. Some almonds
& raisons. he fell on y^e topic of religion
with our 2 good gentlemen, whom he
took for ministers. y^e worst thing he
liked in our religion was y^e putting
up young ladies in Monasteries to be
nuns. at wch you may supose we all
laugh'd heartily. . . .

10th — fair weather & good wind. 5 mile an hour. a Royal dinner & Supper in Comparison of what we have hi=therto had. a form of new regulation drawn up, for ye distribution of our time.

11th — a fine Brisk gale. we Sail'd to day about 9 mile an hour passed over ye mouth of ye Bay Biscay, & pass'd along ye Coast of Spain. miss Nelly & I went up on deck to hail, & get a Sight of ye land of Saints. all Sick at night. ex=cepting our 2 good gentlemen.

12th — A very favorable wind, it Carried us 203 mile in 24 hours. we Sail'd this day along ye Coast of Portugal not Sick ye Captain mended his man=ners giving us a more plentiful dinner to day. all 4 of us Sick.

13th — fine warm weather. a fair wind but very little of it. Sail'd most part of ye day only 2 mile an hour & at most: we reach'd ye rock of Lisbon within about 25 leagues yt is 75 mile. thus we Suppose by degrees, we shall Sufficiently dis=cover ourselves to the world, by getting a peep at all the Countries

round about. as we only intend
Sailing above a 1000 Mile out of
our Way to find the nearest way
home. mrs matthews & miss M: sick
ye others tolerably well.

14th fair weather but very little wind
we saild however about 5 mile an
hour. all tolerably well. saw St Julian
the rock of Lisbon to day. the
Main top gallent mast broke
down but hurt no one in ye fall
mrs matthews had her bed gown
changed into a new fashion'd
sack curiously plaited before
& behind. mr p. gave her the title
of Archdutchess. any one seeing
her fine dress no doubt would
take her for such. ye 2 young
ladies are princesses. but my title
is yet to come. tho our titles in
general are poor babies.

15th a calm of ye coast of Spain. all sick
excepting mrs Neale &c:
16 fine wind & pleasant weather. saild 9 mile an
hour most part of ye day. pass'd the
~~[illegible]~~. Cape St vincents
by the Streits of giberalter. Saild

near 200 mile in ye 24 hours. all poorly mrs Matthews a sore throat: I had ye happiness of pleasing mr p. & for my re=ward got ye title of princess cockle tops or muddle toes.
ye fort St Julien where ye p J. Suffered so much

1790 May ye 1st	We set Sail from ye Texel about 12 o clock with a fair wind. & good weather. we went about 8 mile an hour.
2d Day.	head wind & hard weather, all very Sick except mr noale, who had enough to do, to attend the Sick. we saw yarmouth to day.
3d Day	almost a calm, all ye Sick a little better but Not well. (mr plunket well enough to draw of a keg of gin) & mr neale made us a pot of exellent water chocolate. ye dog & the goat fell down into ye dining room upon ye table, & almost frighten'd mrs Matthews miss nelly & mr plunket out of their witts, thinking perhaps it was the devil. Bob ye cabin boy being there by good luck. hoisted the animal up to ye Captain again (mr neale laugh'd almost to kill him)
4th Day	a calm, obliged to ~~[illegible]~~ come to anchor all tolerably free from Sickness. we Saw Dunkerck Calais & Dover Castle.

we weigh'd Anchor about 7 oclock &
ye Ship toss'd & roll'd about all night
we most of us grew Sick, notwithstan-
-ding a good dish of Chocolate we had
taken of mr plunkets Making. mr

Neale had ye goodness to Sit up till
past 2 o'clock to attend the Sick:

5th Day — Contrary wind. all Sick, except mr
Neale who was our nurse. mr plunket
made us a good pot of Coffee. & ye
Sick managed So as to make a pot of
mull'd wine & took it for their Supper

6th day — head wind & hard weather. all very Sick
except our nurse mr neale, who m..d us
Some wine, & Enquired of ye Sick if they
Cared for any Supper, but took care to
ask them while they were Sleeping.
they no Sooner was awake, & understan-
-ding ye offer yt had been made them
of a Supper. ~~then~~ they Call'd out very
Lustily for Eggs & bacon, wch they eat in
Bed, attended like Sick people. but
laughing very heartily & being very Merry
Bob was ~~to be~~ whip'd for Speaking, we
beg'd him off. but were refused. [illegible]

Writing the Journal by Ship's Lantern.

Rigging on the Ship, 'Brothers'

1790 April the 19 Monday

Set of[f] from Hoogstraet to Breda[1] where we remain'd one night, next morning we went in two car=riages to Utrecht, ↑ lodg'd at a poor house all night. ↓ pass'd by Gorcum a very uncouth place. arrived at amsterdam on the 25th about 4 in the afternoon, we came from Utrecht by water. we Lodg'd at the greatest Inn in town, & paid upwards of 53 flo[rins][2] for 2 days & a half Stay where we made an exhibition of our=Selves, got laugh'd at by all that pass'd us in the Streets, the folks peeping at us under our hats, crying out wat vor een ding is dat.[3] the first night we had so grand & elegant a Supper th[a]t good mr neale could not eat for vexation; the 2 following↑days↓both our gentlemen went out to seek a dinner, whilst we remain'd in all our grandeur, with the best of every thing, attended by Servants at our Backs. the figure we made was highly diverting.

1790 April the 24th Saturday	We took a yeat[4] & Sail'd to the texel,[5] where we arrived about 12 o clock Sunday noon. we were all Sick in the yeat excepting mr Neale. we Lodg'd in it all night & a very unpleasant Lodging we found. we came on board the Ship call'd the Brothers commanded by Captain Mack=duggle,[6] who was not then arrived, he came on Wednesday with 6 passengers a man his wife & 3 small children. 2 maids,[7] Such a Set of Low Lived quarrelsome geniuses as before we never met with. the accomodations we found were very well as to the room, having one entirely to ourselves. the Captain afforded us Subject of trial from his Stingy dirty dispositions. his ill breeding, want of attention &c. the Steward was a Catholic much too good for[8] his Master.
1790 May the 1st	We came on board Sunday the 25 of April. We Set Sail from the texel about 12 o clock[9] with a fair wind. & good weather. We went[10] about 8 mile an hour.
2d Day.	head wind, hard weather. rough sea all Sick but our good conductor mr Neale, who both nurs'd us, & laugh'd at us, in return ↑as he Said↓ for our laughing at him in his great troubles & perplexities at Amsterdam. we saw Yarmouth.[11]
3d Day	almost a calm, all the Sick a little better but not well. mr plunket well enough to draw of a keg of gin. & mr neale made us a pot of excellent water chocolate. the dog & the goat fell down into the dining room upon the table, & almost fright=en'd mrs Matthews miss nelly & Mr plunket out of their wits, thinking perhaps it was the devil. Bob the cabin boy being there by

good luck hoisted the animals up to the Captain again. mr neale laugh'd almost to kill himself.

4th Day A calm, obliged to come[12] to anchor all tolerably free from Sickness. we saw Dunkerck Calais & Dover Castle[13] we weigh'd anchor about 7 o clock am the Ship toss'd & roll'd about all night we most of us grew Sick, notwithstan=ding a good dish of chocolate we had taken of mr plunkets making. mr Neale had the goodness to Set up till past 2 o clock to attend the Sick.

5th Day Contrary wind. all Sick, except mr Neale who was our nurse. mr plunket made us a good pot of coffee. & the Sick managed So as to make a pot of mull'd wine & took it for their Supper

6th Day head wind and hard weather. all very Sick except our nurse mr neale, who m .. d us some wine, and enquired of the Sick if they cared for any Supper, but took care to ask them while they were Sleeping. they no Sooner was awake, & understan=ding the offer that had been made them of a Supper. then they call'd out very Lustily for eggs & bacon, w[hi]ch they eat in Bed, attended like Sick people. but laughing very heartily & being very merry Bob was whipd for Stealing, we beg'd him off. but were refused. &c. &c.

7th a calm upon the coast of nor=mandy.[14] the Sick much better, they made an apple pye rather of the conventual kind, w[hi]ch how=ever might have been pretty good, had the black cook known how to have baked it enough. but it came on the table with the paste half dow & the apples half raw. mr plun: at the expense of a deal of trouble made us a good pot of coffee. & mr neale as usual kind enough to give us up his Share miss Matthews merrily drank our healths in a glass of gin grog, w[hi]ch Seem'd to go down pretty Sweetly for want of Something better... we call'd for Eggs for our supper & after waiting for [th]em about 2 hours & a half, we fell to [th]em with very keen appetites, Dividing an Egg between 2. w[hi]ch by the by was more than good mr neale got the night before, for he came of[f] w[i]th only about a quarter of one to his Share, & glad was he to accept of a piece of bacon we had hid for him in a corner of a Dirty hankerchief. we were remarkeably merry over our Eggs when behold our mirth damp'd all on a sudden by means of a Silly woman who came to us with tail of a tub, frightened out of her Senses, telling us we were in danger of perishing. w[hi]ch news made us fall to our prayers & promises. but it happen'd to prove a false alarm & to our great joy we were assured there had been no danger at all.

N.B. we had Each of us 3 Eggs a piece except miss nelly & myself who had 2 a piece & divided the 3d.

8th — fair wind & weather. a fishing boat came on board, the captain bought 4 cods some mackeral fresh [?] herrings & a fine Scate. we had a very Scanty dinner↑of it,↓& mr neale took care to tell the captain in plain terms at public table th[a]t we had not Enough, th[a]t he expected more. the open, but just complain[t][15] hurt the Captain, he made Some hobling excuse Saying the cook was Sick, but assured mr neale th[a]t he would give him a royal Supper. We were all well to day mrs. matthews excepted who was rather indisposed. I wrote a line to torre abbey.[16]

9th — this morning we pass'd by oussant[17] with a fair breeze & fine weather [,] cross'd the mouth of the bay biscay Entered into the atlantic ocean on our way to Spain, going 8 or 9 mile an hour. a Scanty fish dinner tho' a Sunday. we expect some bacon & eggs for Supper, but very likely shall be disapointed. the Captain to make amends we Suppose for his Stingi=ness at dinner, treated us in the afternoon with a glass of medera Some almonds, & raisons. he fell on the topic of religion with our 2 good gentlemen, whom he took for ministers. the worst thing he liked in our religion was the putting up young ladies in monasteries to be nuns. at w[hi]ch you may supose we all laugh'd heartily.

10th — fair weather & good wind. 5 mile an hour. A royal dinner & Supper in comparison of what we have hi=therto had. a form of new regulations drawn up, for the distribution of our time.

11th — a fine Brisk gale. we Sail'd to day about 9 mile an hour got over the mouth of the Bay Biscay, & pass'd along the coast of Spain. miss nelly & I went up on deck to hail, & get a Sight of the land of Saints. all Sick at night ex=cepting our 2 good gentlemen.

12th — a very favorable wind, it carried us 203 mile in 24 hours. we Saild this day along the coast of portugal[18] The captain minded his man=ners giving us a more plentiful dinner to day. all 4 of us Sick.

13th — fine warm weather. a fair wind but very little of it. Saild most part of the day only 2 mile an hour 5 at most: we reach'd the rock of Lisbon within about 25 leagues that is 75 mile. thus we Suppose by degrees, we shall sufficiently dis=cover ourselves to the world, by getting a peep at all the countries round about. as we only intend Sailing above a 1000 Mile out of our way, to find the nearest way home.[19] mrs matthews and miss M: Sick. the others tolerably well.

14th — fair weather but very little wind. we Saild however about 5 mile an hour. all tolerably well. we saw the rock of Lisbon to day.↑the fort of St. Julian↓[20] the main top gallant mast broke down but hurt no one in the fall Mrs. Matthews had her bed gown changed into a new fashion'd Sack curiously pleated before and behind. mr p. gave her the title of archbishop, anyone Seeing her fine dress no doubt would take her for such. the 2 young ladies are princesses, but my title is yet to come. tho our titles in general↑are poor↓Babies.

15th — a calm of[f] the coast of Spain. all Sick excepting Messr[21] Neale & p:.

16 — fine wind and pleasant↑weather↓ Saild 7 mile an hour most part of the day. passed the cape St. vincents by the Straits of giberaltor. Saild near 200 mile in the 24 hours. all poorly mrs Matthews a↑cold &↓Sore throat: I had the happiness of pleasing mr p. & for my re=ward got the title of princess cockle toes or mu<..>le toes.

1790 May the 17 — fine weather, fair wind. Saild 9 mile an hour. mrs Matthew's cold very Indifferent. the rest of us tolera=bly well. a pilate fish was Seen attending our Ship for Some hours.

the 18th — fair wind. the weather beautiful. Saw the Land. the territory of the king of Morocca in Barbary. on the Coast of Affrica. Mrs Mat=thew's throat very poorly. We made above 240 mile within the 24 hours

the 19th — fair weather, very high winds for these↑Southern↓ Latitudes, rough Sea. Expec=ting to See Land, but Saw none. very near the Coast of affrica. we made more than 200 mile. Us 4 n[uns] very Sick. the Captain much troubled at not Seeing Land.

the 20th — in the morning rough Sea, high winds, Saw the Canary Islands at about 3 leagues distance. the Island of Lancelot, & fort avanture belonging to Spain.[22] at night we were becalmed.[23] all Sick but the 2 good gentlemen, but more Sick of the vulgarity & ill breeding of the Captain. march ramsen &c & the 3 perpetual Squaling children.

the 21 — pass'd in Sight of the grand canary had a Sight of the piek of Teneriffe. was becalm'd the greatest part of the day, at night it blew hard Contrary wind.↑All↓Sick as usual. a terrible rowl-ing night. the Islands a very curious prospect.

the 22d Saturday — Contrary wind tossing & rowling about from one place to another. All very Sick. we Saw within a mile the Island of Teneriffe. a very curious romantic pros=pect. a Sight of the

Steeples & the port of Santa cruce. Some disagreeable gusts of wind. rough Sea & very little advancement. only made about 12 mile in 2 days by contrary winds.

N.B. a remarkeable instance of our B[lesse]d Lady's power & protection over us. Labouring to get in to the port of Teneriffe the wind was against us. the Sea boisterous & scarce any hopes of getting in when good mr neale↑about 3 o clock↓came & proposed to us the making a promise to our B[lesse]d Lady. After w[hi]ch & his [24] Litanies being said, he went & pour'd out Some holy water in the Sea, w[hi]ch he had no Sooner done than an imme=diate change ensued, the wind became more favorable, & we safely arrived in the port. with=in the 24 hours, w[hi]ch they had in vain been Labouring for 2 or 3 Days. the captain & other passengers not knowing what [?] we had done in private, were much astonish'd at the Sudden change & Express'd it Several times after their reaching the port. we were afterwards inform'd, that the people on Shore↑said they↓had never Seen a Ship beat up in such a Manner against the waves.

the 23d pentecost day about 2 o clock we got into port. by the assistance of a Captain of another Ship that lay in harbour. our giddy brain'd Captain lost his bill of health, but providentially it was not calld for, otherwise we should have↑been↓obliged to have kept a quarantain before they would↑have↓ let us gone[25] on Shore. Our Captain went on Shore w[i]th the other Captain, & related to him our history in full tho' we thought it a Secret to him. & in a few hours it was blown↑about↓& spread all over the Island, that 4 nuns[26] had

Escaped from their Monastery & 2 priests running away with them.

the 24th mr p: went on Shore & there heard our history. Mr P. Spoke to the curate who had already heard the report, but very cu=rious to dive into the bottom of our history. he ask'd if we came with the authority of the Apostolical See, & if So why did we not go on Shore to Shew it him Mrp: told him we had the authority of our B[isho]p. & if he wanted to see it he might come himself on board w[hi]ch was more proper, than we to go on Shore, who knew hardly how to walk, being only accustomd to↑walk↓the Cloister &c. Mr p: told him the true account, & said much in favour of the business, Endeavor'd to convince him of the real truth & told him he left it to his prudence to relate it to others in order to suppress the calumny, as far as he could the curate ap̄eard Satisfied with mr p: relation. We had some views of going on Shore to hear M. &c. but were deter'd by the appre=hension of being taken up by the Inquisition, on account of the above mention'd report, in w[hi]ch we Easily conceived there was more ignorance than malice. had we come here to found the good curate might with reason have call'd us to an account for it, but the case being otherwise we did not see↑with↓what authority he could make such a demand. Mr. N. staid at home to guard the 4 renegate nuns. We had a d<...> of laughing among ourselves. mr. N. sick to night.[27]

the 25th nothing very particular. the captain in all respects, as dis=agreeable & as Stingy as ever. all the passengers with good reason much discontended with him, & disgusted with all his bragging & flummery [?] speeches. Mr. P. went on shore & brought us some ↑goat↓ milk extraordinarily good, we made our Suppers of it. We get nothing↑from the cap' unless we ask↓for it, & then 'tis about an Egg[,] or half an Egg apiece, w[hi]ch we sometimes have 2 hours to wait for. w[he]n Sick we once Sent for another Lump of Sugar, the captain Sent it, but bid the Boy tell us there was no more. we have So many instances of his narrow heartedness as w[e]d take up too much time & paper to relate one half. Mr. N. not well & like a fish out of water.

26th Mr. P. Cap: Toby. our Cap: all went on Shore. Mr Ramsen sat in the Capt:s place performing the ceremonies of the table. he helped us So largely to the Bief & pullet, that there was no=thing, but the bare bone left for the cap:s Supper as was the case last night. we are still laying at anchor, in the port of S. Cruce. A garrison town. all longing to Sail for our destind home. tho' in the expectation of many crosses & trials, w[hi]ch have not hitherto been wanting to us. Mr. p. return'd on board at about 8 oclock in the Even brought us some lemons[,] very fine ones[,] a present from Mr. Rooney the gentleman at whose house he dined. he bought several kind of sweetmeats cakes &c. made by the poor Clares Living about 4 mile of[f] the town of S. Cruce. 2 beautiful glass mass cruits[28] & dish with the n[ames] J[esus] & m[ary] on them in letters of gold. We were all very merry over our treasures, & with great alacrity Set to work to erect an alter in mr N. little cabin bed. hung a Linen Sheet all round it. pin'd up the cards. placed a little cross & Steps of mr neales making. two boxes &c. was the alter. a piece of crimson damask for the anti=pendium. a little wax candle cut in two, put up in 2 wine Bottles. the little pretty cruits. Mrs Matthews being too much fatigued with Standing &c. grew very Sick, ↑&↓vomited. we had been remarkeably chearful, mr N. was our chief divertion, while all we did or Said was a pro=vocation to him.

the 27 Mr N. Set up all night to wake us at 3 in the morning for mass that all might be over before the crew was Stir=ring. he then Said M[ass] & we all had the happiness to com[munica]te at it. After a Short recollection we were all very busy putting down our alter, putting the things away. all was Extremely clear'd away↑long↓before 6. the Captain went a Shore, & promis'd to Send us a Leg of mouton for dinner, w[hi]ch we waited for till 3 o clock, find=ing th[a]t none came,[29] Ship mate offer'd us a Bief stake w[hi]ch proved to be Bief and pullet. Mr P. went a Shore in the morn: came home for dinner & brought us a present of 13 Bottles of Mamsey wine from Mr Rooney. bought us a handsome necessary throne [?], with corks[,] Biscuits[,] 2 pretty little alter candlesticks & other articles placed up very care=fully in the pot: after dinner we made ourselves a jug or a pitcher of coffee (for want of a coffee pot.) Just as we were going to take it; in comes the gentleman our benefactor, & paid us a Short & friendly visit, behaving in a most polite & civilized manner. took a dish of coffee & glass of wine with us, expressing his pleasure in having had a Sight of us. if he had before any prejudices at least they seem'd to be all vanish'd. the captain came a board in the even: & we set sail the same night, from S. Cruce.

the 28th Friday — Not much wind, made but little advancement. at three o clock they put on the table a small Plate of fish, a↑little↓bit of the tail & the Shoulder part of a Salted cod, a deal more bone than fish, th[a]t was meant for dinner while the rest had meat. Mr N. ask'd the Cap: if th[a]t was all the fish, he answered yes. mr N. rightly judging it not half Enough for a meal, made us 4 Eat meat, cap: toby & himself made their dinner of the Small bit of fish, Scarce Enough for those 2, mr P. Eat as we did. W[he]n all were Seated Mr N. told the Cap: he had a petition to make in the name of his company & all the passengers. w[hi]ch was to have the dinner at a more reasonable hour, at the half past one, as the waiting So very long, made us all Sick. the Cap: promis'd it Should be at an Earlier hour betwixt one & two. w[hi]ch he thought Early E=nough.

N.B. when the Cap: was on Shore he made a purchase of an old Ram, w[hi]ch I Suppose he Design'd for a choice Delicate bit for us, on Some Extraordinary day. Bief & pullet, has been the chief of our Diet these 4 Last Days, & when it will be otherwise is more than we can tell.

29th — fair wind & good weather. all pretty well. Bief & pullet for dinner. a small bit for Each one. 2d course half a kid roasted, not larger than half a large hair w[hi]ch was to be divided between 11 people. mr N. sup'd with us for A wonder, took a few Slices of cucum=bers & a Biscuit.

N.B. tis to be noted that our < - > Stool is the most Elegant piece of furniture th[a]t is in our whole cabin.

30th Trinity Sunday — We rose at 5. dressed up a little alter, & for the 1st time used our pretty candlesticks. We had not the Benefit of Mass but mr N. consecrated a suf=ficiency of hosts to serve us the rest of the voiage. as he saw no probability of being able to celebrate any more on board. we had however the happiness of com[munion], Mr N. gave com[munion] to mr P. & us 4. then mr P. put on the rochet & Stole & gave it to mr N. after w[hi]ch we made our recollection & then clear'd all away. as Every thing of this nature is a profound Secret there being no Catholicks on board but the Steward who was not present nor knew any thing of the mater. fine day. good wind. made a tolerable advancement tho' have yet above 32 hundred miles to go. all pretty well.

31st — fair wind. all pretty well. they kill'd the old Ram. they had a fry of the Liver & Sides for Supper. Mr N. said twas the best thing he had Eat Since a board this Ship. Every day brings new instances of the cap: miserly Disposition, his conversation runs commonly on Noblemen Lords Ladies &c. with whom he pretends to have been very intimate, but has nothing at all of a gentleman or any appearance of it in his behaviour. he knows nothing but abusive Language to all under his authority, Swea=ring & cursing is as customary↑to him↓as his Speaking. infine his whole conduct is Such as twill be won=derful if he is not ruin'd, for both Sailers & passengers have Enough to take hold of him for the Sailers declare had it not been for cap: toby who they are fond of they wou'd have left the Ship. They are already put to an allowance of bread. 1 Small loaf aday. the cap: Seeing us at work Said our cabin look'd like a man < - > mak<...> Sho<..>.

31st — the Cap: kick'd the Steward in the face, giving him as he allways dos shameful abusive Language. its all of apiece we have not Spoons Enough for Tea nor dinner but must wait till others have done, & for his part he is rude Enough to Eat out of the nasty wooden Ladle & helps others with it again after he has Lick'd it. he praises & commends every thing th[a]t comes upon the table as the most Extraordinary thing in the world. & is his own trumpetter in Every thing Else

June the 1st — fair wind, & weather, made a great deal of advancement. the famous Ram came upon table & proved the best mouton we had Eat on board this Ship. tho' we dreaded it thinking it wou'd be mouton & pullit however we were all agreeably disap̄ointed. the cap: paid us a comp[lemen]t th[i]s evening at the tea w[hi]ch certainly deserves notice. he Said he Should like to have us for passen=gers again, for he has never had Such good Luck before,[30] had never gone above 4 or 5 mile an hour[,] where as Since we have been on board he has Sail'd 8 9 nay 10 mile an hour. whether he Said as he thought we cannot tell, at least Such was his comp[lemen]t. all tolerably well.

2d — wind Still very favourable make a deal of advancement. from yesterday 12 till to day 12 made 172 mile. all pretty well. th[i]s Evening the wind Seems to have fallen a little. but hope it will Soon rise again. Mrs Ramsen call'd in our room to See us & after Looking about her for a while, Seeing us at work Said, this Looks like a Sowing School. She brought her work basket, & ask'd us leave to come & Sit with us but we told her the Steward was coming to Sweep She took the hint & away She walk'd

3d we had the happiness of going to com[muni]on, the Same hour as before. mr neale receiv'd it from mr P. after having given it to us. the weather fine wind fair, some part of the day was almost a calm. I was dressed in a fine Silk petticoat & a chince jacket th[a]t had been given me in alms - w[hi]ch was So becoming & made me look So Extraordinarily fine th[a]t all my companions were jealous of me.

4th good weather, but little wind not much advancement: Mr Neale troubled with a sad pain in his back. Miss nelly desires me not to fail marking down a remarkeable Sentance of one of the Sailers. viz th[a]t he believed the fine weather was owing to the Ladies below. we were all Sick. the Cap: out of great consideration offer'd us to make some fine tea among ourselves, & to send us a tea kettle of boiling water. we made it of↑the↓fine green tea he gave us a week or 2 ago. they were all very merry in the cabin at night Singing & playing musically upon their glasses. we heard them from our own room, where us 4 allways Sup together, when we can get any thing to Sup upon.

5th wind & weather as yesterday all pretty well. cap: toby caught a Dolphin. Mr N's back worse no Sleep all night. he attributes his backach to our taking vani=ty in the Cap: & Sailers compliment he thinks it a little hard th[a]t we

S[houl]d lay the burden of our pride up[on] his poor back. the falling of the wind is also look'd upon as the consequence of our vanity.↑mr Neale & the cap: laid a wager mr N. laid we See the coast of am[erica] in 16 Days.↓

6th fair weather, mr N's back a little better. the rest pretty well all but mr P. who is indisposed[.] being Sunday we perform'd our Devotions as usual rising at 5 o clock. when all was ready & mr N. going to Strike a light there was not a bit of tinder to be found in the box, w[hi]ch Sur= prised us not a little it apearing as if old Scratch had taken it away to deprive us of Com[mu-ni]on, as he had also Endeavour'd to do the last time by hiding the tinder box in Mr N. night cap.

7th fair wind, good weather all↑4↓pretty well. Mr Neales Back a little better. Mr p: but poorly.

8th fair weather, fine brisk breezes[31] went 6 mile an hour; in the 24 made 112. mr N: & mr P. better. the rest pretty well. while we were conversing upon old monastical affairs & our [?] private concerns, down falls the hog into our room upon the table. the Dog had been worying it. Miss Matthews fared the worst for the hog Scrambled till he rowl'd[32] in her lap She tossed him down & was not a little Startled to find Such an unwellcome guest so near her we were all more frightend than hurt. our Surprise being over we all laugh'd very heartily & the Scene Ended in merriment

9th almost a calm some time of the day[.] made in

all about 100 mile. - Mr N. back very poorly the rest tolerably well.

10th — went to our Devotions as usual the devil did not meddle with the tinder box th[i]s morning, all was found in form & order.

11th — the wind fair but not much of it. a Squal of wind towards night for a Short time. mr Neales knee & leg bad. the rest pretty well.

12th Saturday — fair wind, about 12 o clock began a fine brisk gale th[a]t carried us 150 mile in the 24 hours. mr N. pains Still very great; mrs Matthews knee Swell'd & very painful we Supose it to be the Rhumatism w[hi]ch She has probably catch'd from going bare kneed th[a]t is to Say her Stocking legs were So lose th[a]t they would not keep up.

13th — the fine brisk wind con=tinues, Sometime in the day Saild above 8 mile an hour. Our morning ↑ Devotions ↓ perform'd as usual: Mr N. Something better in the morning grew worse at night Mrs matthews knee very Stiff & painful. the rest very well. & in good Spirits hoping Soon to reach our journeys End.

14th — fair wind, good weather, mr N. & mrs Matthews Rhuma=tism better. the rest well[.] Sour cakes for breakfast. ↑Saild 108↓

15th — fair wind, Saild 151 mile. hard, Sour, musty cakes for breakfast. Mr N. better able to wish [?] the Cap:s head for his rudeness & incivility to him at Dinner. mrs Matthews better. the rest well

16th very little wind. Mr N. better mrs Matthews tolerable, the rest well.

17th almost a calm. we said our Ladys Litanies to obtain a good Breese. the Steward brought down the Soupe. was just Setting it on the table when the handle of the turine broke Spilt all the Soupe a great part of w[hi]ch fell upon mrs Matthews petticoat the rest upon the ground mr ramsen was so griev'd at the loss of the soupe that he told the cap: if he would whip [?][33] the Steward he would hold him the while. we had the happiness to per=form as usual our devotions this morning. at about the half past 5. mr N. & Mrs Mat: almost well. the rest tolerably So.

18th a Dead Calm. all tolerably well. Short in all kind of provisions

19th Almost a Calm: our Captain & cap' - toby went on board a Sloop coming from America bound to the West Indies,[34] he went to get provisions but came back only with a Small bag of Brown biscuits refusing the offer of other kind of provisions, Saying he had plenty on board, while we all by Sad experience knew to the contrary, there being Scarce any white Biscuits left. No more brown Sugar very few candles, < - > or in Short of any other necessary provisions.[35] [...] Neptune came on board & made Sport among the Sailers We gave Each of us 4, half a crown a head. Miss Mat↑& <..>↓very Sick.

20. A Dead Calm. all pretty well.

21
St aloy
sius

Still a Calm. the Steward fell down the stairs & hurt himself very much. Our Devotions in the morning as usual. Matches & candles like all other provisions almost out. made a devotion to St Aloysius to obtain a Safe & Speedy arrival. all tolerably well.

22d

tolerable brisk wind. good weather made for some hours 5 or 6 mile an hour. came near permoudus,[38] but not in Sight. Mr N. in consequence lost his wager. All tolerably well.

23d

a great Squal of wind began at 6↑in the morning↓& lasted till almost 12 heavy rains, & Excessive high Seas. terrible tossing & rowling about. the fore top mast & top gallant mast[,] the Steering Sails[,] main brases &c.- were carried away by the wind because they were↑not↓taken in in time: tho the cap[tai]n was forewarn d of it by the boat=Swain a while before. the Sailers cursed his conduct, the cook & all the rest laugh'd at his misfortune. they repair'd the old broken top=mast as there was no wood on board to make a new one. the Eggs from Sancte cruce spoilt. rotten Eggs, musty fried ham & stinking mutton for dinner. we Excused th[a]t Suposing it was on account of the great bustle in the morning. the Ship almost Stripd of her Sails, appeard in a very distressed Situation. thank god no one on board was hurt. She was all new painted a few days ago[37] to make a figure at new york for any thing th[a]t we know to the contrary. Miss Matthews Sick the rest tolerably well. pass'd the Island of permoudus[38] without Seeing it. at about 1 o clock afternoon the wind fell & changed almost a head. Saild only about 3 mile an hour.

24th we had not the hapiness of com[muni]on for fear of coming Short. the wind against us in the morning became fair at about 6 in the Evening. the weather very plea=sant. passed the Cape haterass. all pretty well. the cap: very anxious on account of his Short provisions Especially of bread.

25th fair wind & weather. all pretty well. we met a Scotch brig. our cap: went on board ↑of it↓ to beg one bag of bread, when he Shoud have bought half a dozen it proved Sour. the cap of the brig offer'd our cap a whole cheese but he refused it brought only a little bit tho he had Scarce a quarter of a p[oun]d in his Ship. we had for Din-ner a Shoulder of Stinking mutton. tho' he was forewarn'd not to bring it at table on account of its insupporta=ble Stench. mr Neale sent it of[f] the table the moment it came in, the cap: look'd very Silly on it tho' dared not Say any thing about it. we had but a Short dinner.

26th head wind, high Sea, the weather very Squaly. a very Stormy night of wind & rain, all poorly. had Sight of a little Sloop from new london bound to martinick loaded with cattle & horses, we Spoke her but She went on her course & only answerd us once.

27 the weather So rough & Stormy th[a]t we were deprived of the comfort of performing our de=votion, the waves very high th[a]t they broke over the main deck & pour'd down upon us in our little room very plentifully. the Ship creen'd down So low th[a]t the top of the main mast touch'd the water the Ship rowled So th[a]t we coud not possibly keep footing Mrs Matthews & myself fell down but did not hurt

ourselves. a while after I fell again & bruised my=self very much. the night was more moderate all very poorly the Cap for the first↑time↓ came to us & brought us a bit of a relish w[hi]ch he handed us himself & paid us more attention than usual. the gentlemen dined upon deck. our dinner of boild foul & Stinking ham was Sent us below, the Cap: went to bed & gave no orders for Supper for any of his passengers but our gentlemen calld for the cold meat & took care to help↑us &↓themselves.

28th the weather very rough. Squaly & rainy, a deal of tossing & rowling about, a fresh gale all day. about 4 o clock they Sounded & found no bottom.

29th we went to our Devotions as usual. a very brisk gale. thunder & lightning & rain in the morning. at 12 at noon they Sounded & found bottom 80 fathom deep. Sounded again at 8 & found 35. again at 12 at Night & found 30. M: Nelly ↑very↓ill.

30th almost a Calm. they Sounded at 4 in the morning & found 25. Again at 8 & found 30.

N.B. last night we had Some hogs feet & pullet to our Supper. & a bit of hard Salt Bief in the usual Elegant Man=ner one plate one knife & fork among 4. at about 12 there was not a candle to be found for the <...>inacle[39] mr. N. fearing it might be dange=rous to be without a light So near the Shore offerd the cap: 1 of our candles who had the impudence to tell him he had a plenty, tho' we knew he had not one in his Ship. he accepted our candle not=withstanding, his plenty & look'd confused. At about 11 we saw Land, call'd never Sink. a pilate came on board between 5 & 6 in the Evening, conducted us round Sandy hook[40] & cast Anchor. Miss nelly a little better. the rest tole=rably well.

We arrived at New york friday Morning the 2d of July. Lodg'd at one Mrs white. Stay'd there till Sunday the 4th when we saild to norfolk in Capt Cary Sloop arrived there on the friday following[,] the 9th[.] Sat Saild th[a]t Same Evening for Maryland in Capt gibsons Sloop.[41] We landed in charles County on Sunday the 11th & have had vanity of habitation Ever Since.[42]

Mr. plunket left us at new york to tra=vel by land.[43]

34 Boxes & Truncks
belonging to our Company
5 Bags. a Small
port Manteau.
a Small Casse of Brandy.
3 hampers of Wine.
a Little basket a tin box

6 Truncks.
6 Boxes.
~~a Small port manteau~~
a Small Wheel.
a Chamber Conveniency.
2 hampers of Wine,
Containing 5 Douzain of
Bottles each.
a half-quarter Cask of
Wine.
Passengers Baggage all
for Exportation.

Baggage Receipts

The debarkation from Gibson's Sloop

NOTES

1. Hoogstraet or Hoogstraten is a city near the north central border of Belgium in the province of Antwerp. Breda, not more than 15 miles north of Hoogstraten, is a city in the Southern Netherlands in the province of North Brabant.

2. The florin is a European silver coin.

3. The Dutch phrase means: "What kind of a thing is that?"

4. The word intended is "yacht."

5. Texel is one of the West Frisian Islands off the northern coast of Holland in the North Sea.

6. According to Norman Brouwer, the historian of the South Street Seaport Museum in New York, "Brothers" was a 200 ton full rigged ship built in New York in 1776. She had, therefore, three masts with square sails on all three. By 1790 she was British owned and in that year the Lloyds register of London gives among the fifty or so ships called "Brothers" this one owned by Capt. McDougall and Co. She was built of live oak and her voyage is recorded in the registry as from London to New York. D.J. Lyon of the National Maritime Museum in London states: "She was probably a tween decked vessel with proper stern windows, a bow with a figurehead and rails and with both forcastle and poop, which is what frigate normally meant when used to describe a merchant ship." In other words, frigate was another name for a full rigged ship. This means "Brothers" was only loosely connected to the warship type called a frigate.

7. Clare Joseph says six passengers came on board. If there were "2 maids" and "3 children," the family would have totalled seven. "2 maids" is difficult to decipher.

8. Crossed out: "the."

9. There are two texts for May 1-3. The second version adds "noon."

10. Alternate text reads: "sail'd."

11. The alternate text is used here. The original entry reads: "head wind & hard weather, all very Sick Except mr neale, who had Enough to do, to attend the Sick. we Saw yarmouth to day." Great Yarmouth is located in England on the coast of Norfolk, east of Norwich, across the North Sea from Amsterdam.

12. Crossed out: "put out."

13. Dunkirk and Calais in France and Dover in England are seen passing from the North Sea through the Strait of Dover into the English Channel.

14. Before 1790 Normandy was one of the historic provinces of France situated on the English Channel between Picardy on the north and Brittany on the south. In spite of the passing of two centuries, the historic provinces which existed before 1790 still command the local patriotism of most French people.

15. This word could be complaining or complaint.

16. Torre Abbey was situated in the district of Tormoham, in the county of Devon in England. Clare Joseph's cousin, Father John Halford (1753-1806), served there for seventeen years. John was an excellent classical scholar and was the son of Ann Welch (or Walsh) and Thomas Halford, who was probably Clare's Uncle. Correspondence in the Archives of the Carmelite Monastery, Baltimore, shows she had an Uncle G. Halford who lived in Yorkshire.

17. Ushant Island (French: d'Ouessant) is located off the western most coast of France. Up to 1790 this area was part of the historic province of Brittany and is now in the department of Finistere. The Bay of Biscay opens out to the southeast of Ushant Island.

18. Crossed out: "not So."

19. In a letter sent by Mother Bernardina Matthews to her former confessor at Hoogstraet Carmel in 1790 after her arrival in Southern Maryland, she writes: "We had a good voyage and not very long considering the course we passed. The captain deceived us saying he was bound for New York and Philadelphia - but he had taken in a parcel of goods to deliver at Teneriffe, one of the Canary Islands belonging to Spain, which fact we did not know when we engaged him. He sailed down the Southern latitudes which made it very hot and was 2000

miles further than we should have gone had we sailed straight for America." She adds that after leaving Santa Cruce they "sailed the course called the Trades." (From a handwritten copy sent to Baltimore Carmel before 1940. Original is in the archives of Lanherne Carmel in Cornwall, formerly the Carmel of English-Antwerp.)

20. At the bottom of this page Clare Joseph adds a note: "the fort St Julian where the p J suffered so much." In the second half of the eighteenth century, the Portuguese penal system boasted a series of underground dungeons, the most celebrated of which was Sao Juliano. Here, in its tight underground chambers, during the suppression of the Society of Jesus in Portugal, one hundred and eighty Jesuits from the missions were brutally imprisoned by Sebastiao Jose de Carvalho. While the French and Austrian Jesuits were eventually released through their governments' intervention, the Portuguese Jesuits "rotted away through the years. Seventy-nine died in the dungeons; others went mad. Only in 1777...did about sixty survivors emerge after over fifteen years of confinement." William V. Bankert, S.J., *A History of the Society of Jesus,* (St. Louis: Institute of Jesuit Sources, 1972), p. 370-71.

The Carmelites of the Low Countries were apparently very aware of the sufferings of the Jesuits during their exile and suppression in Europe and the missions. In the archives of the Carmelite Monastery in Baltimore, there is a 1760 account written in the hand of Sr. Ann Lewis (or Louisa) Hill, John Carroll's cousin, who was a member of the Carmelite Monastery in Hoogstraet. In 1790 she succeeded Mother Bernardina Matthews as Prioress. Her account details the suppression of the Jesuits in Brazil and the imprisonment of two hundred and sixty of them on "a man of war." They were forbidden to land when they finally reached Lisbon and eventually were put ashore at Civitavecchia in the Papal States.

21. Although it is evident Messr. was meant, the spelling is difficult to decipher.

22. Lanzarote and Fuerteventura are the two Canary Islands sighted by the travelers on May 20.

23. Crossed out: "of the Spanish coast."

24. Crossed out: "& ye."

25. Crossed out: "go."

26. Crossed out: "& 2."

27. This sentence is added in the margin.

28. The Baltimore Carmelites have in their possession one of these cruets. It was taken to the foundation of the Bettendorf, Iowa Carmel in 1911 but later returned to the Baltimore community by one of the foundresses, Mother Aloysius Heiker.

29. Crossed out: "we called for."

30. Crossed out: "again."

31. Crossed out at beginning of entry for the 8th: "what little wind there was < - - >."

32. Crossed out: "fell."

33. This word is crossed out and written over. It could possibly be "stripe" or "whip."

34. The sloop sailing from "America bound to the West Indies" was sighted three days before the travellers on the "Brothers" saw Bermuda and eleven days before American land was sighted coming into New York harbor on July 30th.

35. A small section of the document is cut away here. The missing piece could have held three lines of text. "Neptune..." follows the missing lines.

36. A later correction of this spelling appears as an inter-linear entry in pencil in Clare Joseph's hand and reads: "Bermudas."

37. Crossed out: "before."

38. A spelling correction appears again in pencil in Clare Joseph's hand: "Bermudas."

39. Perhaps "spinnaker" was meant here: a large jib-like sail on the main mast opposite the main sail.

40. Never Sink and Sandy Hook appear on "A Map of the British Empire in America" for 1733. In 1755 the two reappear as Navesink

Hills and Sandy Hook. They can still be found on current maps and are located at the northermost tip of the outer banks of New Jersey at the entrance of Lower New York Bay.

41. The party sailed north from Norfolk, up the Chesapeake Bay to Southern Maryland where they followed the Potomac River to their destination in Charles County.

42. In the letter to her confessor quoted in note no. 19, Mother Bernardina writes: "...on Sunday [Saturday] the 10th we arrived safe at Mr. Boby Brent's landing which is about a mile from my nephew Ignatius' house. It was then too late to land our baggage but we met with a man who was going to fish and we prevailed on him to return to shore with a letter for Mr. Brent and Ignatius to inform them to come to us early in the morning.

Ignatius came off immediately, and came on board our vessel about 10 oclock on Saturday night. He returned to shore however that <-> again, and came to us again on Sunday morning about 5 oclock when we landed with all our baggage and went up to Mr. Brent's where Mr. Neal said Mass about 8 - We dined there and in the evening went over to Nacy's house intending to make that our habitation till a more convenient place could be provided. We remained there 8 days - it was then judged more proper that we should come to Mr. Neal's house by Porto Bacco which was much larger and not inhabited. We put on our Habit the second day of our arrival [July 21] and keep our regularity as well as we can.

A place was agreed on for our Convent in St. Mary's County much to our satisfaction, but some difficulties arose about it, and Mr. Carrol being in England about three weeks before our arrival, his vicar thought proper we should choose another place, and Mr. Baker Brooke has made us a present of his own dwelling with several acres of land round about it to make a Convent of."

43. This entry regarding Plunkett is in the margin beside the undated entry beginning, "We arrived at New York..." Mother Bernardina adds: "...he came to see us since our arrival and is now on the mission."

'Chandler's Hope'

Other Documents:

Regulations for Superiority

Bernardina's Profession

Clare Joseph's Acquitance and verses in praise of the Sisters

A Supr ought to have ye courag without any regard to
human respects or distinction of persons. to exact Equally
of all her religious ye observance of Rules & Disipline.
but wth as much Sweetness & mildness on one side, as
if She beg it as a favour. & on ye other wth ye authority
of a Superiour, yt will be obeyed. thus to maintain
ye integrity of obedience in her Subjects whom She
Shoud never permit to go contrary to wt She thinks fitt
to ordain. if they have any thing to propose against
her orders. She Shoud hear ym wth patience. & if possible
often approve their reasons. but to draw them Sweetly
to obedience. & give ym ye full merit of it without
pretending to answar any of their reasons. but say
Dr Sister yr reasons are very good. I do not dislike what
you propose. but for ye present my Dr Child, let it be
don as I say. & offer up to God ye difficultys in it.
in reprehensions She aught to use ye Same moderation
& Sweetness. & only seek ye amendment of ye faulty
not ye confusion of ye Delinquent. never to reprehend in
motions of passion, or wth a mind & voice agetated.
nor any terms yt can exasperate ye partie. but
allways such as may move ym to be sensible of their
faults & incourage to amend them. after having
Different ways used these perswaves means. to no
effect. then Say wth mildness if such & such a fault
be not mended. or such a thing done wch I ordered.
yu will force me against my will to use Severity
& to give you a pennance. Since it is my obligat
ion to do so, by orders of ye constetutions. wch
is my indispencable Duty to comply with
She must have a great Zeal for ye Spirituall advancemt
of their Religious. & spear no pains for that end

Mary Margaret Brent's 'Regulations for Superiority'

2

whilst at ye same time she must not neglect her own, but Labour to perfect her Self as that of others depends upon hers. She must Sacrifice her rest, repose & Solitude for ye good of others. & procure a little cell within her own heart, where she may often retire to recover a little Spirituall breath, joyning Solicitude & Solitude togather. to be in every place where her Authority is necessary attentive to all ye Necessitys of Each one of ye comminity, to look to her Self; both with regard to Necessarys of all kinds & yt ye Dyet may be in ye best manner accommodated within ye bounds of Religious Poverty. no Superfluities but nothing shoud be deminished of wt ye Rule and Custome allowes. all is to be equelly distributed wth Charity according to justice. ye same shoud be observed in all other Necessarys conveniencies. wch ye Religious are to have either for their own private use or for ye offices they are intrusted with. yt there may be no reasons given for complaints. or of absenting themselves from publick dutys. or acts of community. tho ye whole concerns of ye house, both Spiritual & temporals, rests upon ye shoulders of ye Supr., yet it shoud not be taken in ye sence yt she is to make it her duty, to do all ye particular offices of ye house her Self. but only to see yt they are performed according to ye Spirit of ye order. & conformable to ye constitutions. for this it is not necessary, to be runing into all corners of ye house. to be couriously prying into every ones businefs. ordering here & there. & perhaps counter ordering ye next moment wch will ocation great confusion & disturbance.

3

to ye community. & particularly to those in ye offices
who see by ys proceeding, they can not be trusted in wt
belongs to their office. without being suspected by their
Supr, wch is a thing attended wth such bad consequences
yt she will never be Lov'd nor obey'd. nor will ye Subjts
ever have any confidence in her, besides such a way
of acting is beneath ye dignity of a Supr. who ought
to have more confidence in ye Vertue of their Subjects.
then to think yt they woud not do their duty - unless
she was at their Elbows. she ought to be nor chainte
yet to be upon ye watch to surprise them in a fault.
yt she might have an occasion to exert her
authority. or make a show of her zeal. yet she sd.
now & then visit ye offices, & inform her self how
they are performed. wth wt spirit & charity &c. & if
nothing was wanting - & to order proper remedys.
&c. if any thing be amiss.

another dangerious & difficult point. wch regards
ye office of superiority. & ought caarfully to be looked
too. wch is to avoid wth equall care. ye too much
Indulgence on one side. & too much severity on ye
other. both Equally pernicious to ye Supr themselves
& distructive of regularity & good discipline in ye
Subjects. it may be compar'd to too dangerous Rocks,
who lye so close by one another. & have so narrow a
passag between ym - yt requires a skillfull & experi
enced Pilote to guid ye Vessel much to steadiness between
both, as not to split upon one. through too much
Eagerness of avoiding ye other. but by dexterity &
prudence to go directly in ye middle between ye
two extreams. of severity & indulgences that
she may never be feared for too much of ye first.
nor slighted for any excess of ye second. but be
Eaquely respected. Eaquely beloved. & Eaquely obey'd
by her Subjects. whether she shows ye septer of command
or sword of justice.

She aught to help ym. to bear their burdens: in hiding from their eys. like a tender Mother. ye rigiours wch ye Sword of justice requires. by doing her duty, as reason & prudence dictates. & alway to remember she is not Superiour for her Self. but for her Subjects. who has all theire dependance upon her both Spiritual & temporall. to reflect yt others were as worthy of it, & more so, then her Self yt neither she nor any else. has any other right to ye preferance. yn ye free Election of ye Comty. She sd consider yt ye very title of Rd Mot. wch puts ye relegions in mind of ye respect, reverance & obedience due to her. so it aught to put her in mind of ye love, tenderness. & compassion she owes to them. & to be continualy mindfull of ye Lesson. of our Devine Master. to learn of me, because I am meek & humble of heard. so to lay a Side intierly. all Soverain. haughty, imperious, & dispotick way of acting. wch is odious in a Secular person. & much more so, in a religious. they sd command wth resolution & stedyness as occations requires. but at ye same time, wth so much sweetness. affability. & even humility. yt they coud not but love ye command. because they coud not forbar loveing ye person yt commanded. the Supr may & aught to do this. wth ye aime of gaining ye affection of theire Subjects not for ye Satisfaction of being beloved. wch is neither to be Sought nor desired. but by such means she may sweetly bring ym to be more in love wth theire Rule & duty, so to increas theire Love to God.
on ye other hand she must prudently consider. yt to wink at all faults. & to grant all requests without distinctions is not only to bring authority into contempt. but to extinguish all fervour & devotion, turning Rule & discipline into relaxation. it is in a word, to distroy religion & spiritual government

regular observance dos not consist in allwas punishing
or allways Sparing - but in prudently judging according
to ye different circumstances of time & place. disposit=
ons of persons & ye like. yt is, wn it is time to punish - when
to Spare - wn to refuse, & wn to grant - never to use
severity when Sweetness will do - nor neve to use indulgence
when it wou'd do more harm then good. for all this, great pruden[ce]
is necessary - to endevour to rule over ye hearts of their
Subjects - more then over theire persons - to make theire
obedience as Sweet to ym as if they were doin their
own wills by doing hers - or rather ye will of God - under her
direction. & after her example -
if a Supr through theire neglect - or weakness in condescend-
ing. connives at breaches of Rules & discipline, so as to
occation any considerable disorder, Irregularity, or
Laxity to creep into an order - or Religious Comty -
every Subject must answer themselves for theire guilt
in these breaches .. but ye Super must answer for all & for
this reason Authority is given them - yt haveing power
to punish & correct delinquents, they may have no
Excuse at Gods tribunal. if through too much indulgence
faults are left unpunished, & therefore never mended.
the great Art of governing in Religion consists in ye
right use of yr Authority, that is - in a seasonable
mixture of mildness & severity, wch are two qualitys
necessary in all Superiours. the excess of Either makes
them equally guilty in ye sight of God, because both are
Equally distructive of discipline & good order, too much
mildness destroys it directly, [illegible] & too much
Severity destroys it inderectly, by destroying charity in
ye hearts of ye inferiours. without wch it can never
Subsist - they must joine ye tenderness of a mother with the
authority of a Superiour

6

they must joyne ye tenderness of a Mother with the Authority of a Superiour. yt whilst ye Subjects love her admirable sweetness, in quality of a tender Mother. they at ye same time respect her, as ye most awfull of Superiours.
because she aught to be resolute in requireing exact observance, more particularly in points of Vertue.
Not suffering ye least erregularity of yt kind to pass without due satisfaction. accepting when such faults happen through mistake. surprise, or a first motion. but not when a habit custom. malice, or any obstinacy of will or judgment is ye cause of it. no quarter shoud be given in ys case. after ye first, second, or third, admonection. but all correction must be in ye spirit of charity, meekness & all ye sweetness yt can possible be made use of. in ye occation.
Zeal for exact observance of Rules & constetutions aught allways to be active in a Supr. because god him self is ye Author of all Religions Institutions. & the Rules are ye dictates of ye holy Ghost. & also because the happiness of all those, whom God so specially calls to serve him in ye perfect way of Liveing under those Rules, intirely depend upon ye exact observance of them. & consequently they concern him as nearly as his honour, & theire happiness can do.
Now as ye good opperation of a nice piece of work, is no small commendation to ye workman yt made it. & an ill operation, or any disorder in ye parts yt compose it. not only reflects upon ye Author, but even indangers ye whole work, so we may say yt if Almighty God is highly honoured by Religions, wn Rules & discipline is well observed. he is Equally dishonoured, wn it is neglected. because the scandal thereby given. not only makes people often blame ye Institution of wch he is ye Author. but als exposs ye Religions it self to ruin. & distruction.

Profession of Bernardina.

I Bernardina Therese Xaveria of St Joseph Make my Profession and Promis Obedience Chastity & Poverty unto Almighty God and to the Blessed virgin Mary of Mount Carmell and to the Reverend Lord Bishop of Antwerp Dominick and to his Successours according to the first Rule of the said order without Mittigation untill Death.

Bernardina Therese Xaveria of St Joseph

This Profession was made the 30 of September 1755 in the Monastery of our Lady of Sicham of the English Religious women of the order of Saint Therese. in Hoogstrate in the hands of the Right Reverend Mother Isabella Mary Joseph of the Holy Ghost Prioress of the foresaid Monastery with Express Leave of the Most Illustrious and Reverend Lord Bishop of Antwerp Dominick. The Said Sister was Native of Maryland born in Charles County in the world She was Called Ann Matthews Daughter to Mr Joseph Matthews by his wife Susana Craycroft Daughter to Mr Ignatius Craycroft. the Said Sister made her Profession when She was in ye 23 year of her Age She brought to the Monastery 150 £ Ster

Isabella Mary Joseph of ye Holy Ghost Prioress
Mary Ann of Jesus Subprioress

Antwerp April ye 12th 1790.

For My Separating from the English Carmelites
Of Antwerp to go to found in America. I acknowledge
to have received from the Superiour & Comunity
Of the Said Convent, the Sum of one hundred
pounds Sterling, All due in payment for the same
Sum given at My Profession in the year 1773.

Witness My hand Clare Joseph of
the Sacred Heart of Jesus.
Alias) Frances Dickinson

Frances Heart of J: Pro vd
Prioress

Philipine M of St Xav: Subprioress
Teresa Maria of the Holy Ghost. D.
Mary Xaveria of the Angels D.

Sig: Clares Dickenson;
acquitance when
she went to Mary-land